The Happy Addict

How to be Happy in Recovery from Alcoholism or Drug Addiction

by

Beth Burgess

First published in the UK in 2013

Published by Eightball Publishing

ISBN 978-0-9573217-1-7

Copyright © 2013 Beth Burgess

About the Book

If you are an addict who has got clean and sober, and you are now looking to take the next steps to improve your life, this book is for you.

Many people put down the drink or drugs, but are still struggling to be happy and healthy. *The Happy Addict* teaches you how to overcome the hurdles that often face us in recovery, and how to use your experience of addiction for good.

This book will show you different ways of thinking and being, so you can have positivity and peace of mind, along with your sobriety.

This is an essential book for anyone who feels their recovery could always be improved.

About the Author

Beth Burgess is a Life and Recovery Coach and the founder of Sort My Life Solutions (Smyls) Coaching & Consulting.

Her missions include helping as many people as possible to achieve an amazing recovery and ending the stigma toward people with addictions.

She is the also the author of *The Recovery Formula: An Addict's Guide to getting Clean and Sober Forever.*

Visit Beth at http://www.smyls.co.uk

Contents

To all the other addicts who showed me love, acceptance, support and encouragement.

And for showing me recovery.

Introduction

I don't know about you, but all the alcoholics and drug addicts I have met are lovely people. They're funny, they're insightful and they have a unique ability to look at personal tragedy with a certain black humour. For the most part, they tend to be sensitive and intelligent individuals, with big hearts. Well, that's when they've stopped drinking and drugging obviously.

In fact alcoholics and drug addicts often have some nicer qualities than their more 'normal' peers. Recovering addicts can be much less judgemental than people you might find in other walks of life; they tend to be more empathetic - and *man*, they're strong people. To live through an addiction, survive and come out on the other side, despite all your problems, you have got to be of strong character.

In my opinion, recovering alcoholics and drug addicts are a special breed of people; but the problem is, they often don't believe that. If you're anything like me, you may well accept the previous comments to be true of all the other alkies and druggies you encounter, but you don't see it in yourself.

That was my own personal experience for a long time. I had huge respect for other people in recovery, but I hated myself and I didn't think I was as good as them. Thankfully, I have worked on myself - and I now respect my own recovery in the same way that I respect that of others.

Now that I am sober and work as a Recovery Coach, I spend a lot of time with recovering alcoholics and drug addicts - and I am always dismayed to see people who may be several years sober still being hard on themselves, still not fully embracing life, and finding

9

it hard to move on. Of course it is important to be vigilant about making mistakes, and to always be aware of your weaknesses, but not to the extent that you punish and limit yourself; not to the extent that you hold yourself back from developing all your positive qualities and becoming someone amazing. And sadly I see that a lot - people not enriching their lives as much as they truly deserve to, because they believe certain negative things about themselves.

It is unfortunate, because all the recovering addicts I see have so many unique qualities and skills - and yet they either don't see them, or they're so held back and limited by their own beliefs about themselves that they're scared to seek success.

Proponents of some addiction recovery methods may tell us recovering addicts to stay quiet, be humble, hide your problems away; maybe in an effort to pretend the past hasn't happened. Or they may make us feel ashamed of ourselves and of our shortcomings. They sometimes tell us to be patient and just wait for the pain to heal. But how can you heal and recover fully if you are hiding away all the time, mired in shame, and effectively denying your past?

It's time to be proud of yourself, and what you've achieved by stopping drinking or taking drugs. You can share this sense of achievement and joy with whoever else you like, but it is extremely important that you acknowledge it to yourself and that you *live* it.

And before any of you start protesting that we are supposed to be humble and avoid stroking our own egos in recovery, this book is not suggesting that you run around telling everyone how fantastic you are. This isn't about baseless pride; it is about acknowledgement, acceptance, gratitude and the celebration of recovery.

You can live an incredible life, and become an amazing person quite humbly. In fact, what better way to show your gratitude for your sobriety and for what you have now than by doing this very thing?

The mistake most people make when they are trying to recover from addiction is that they see the past as one big mess that they want to put behind them. Many recovering alcoholics and drug addicts have a sense that they would like to atone for any wrongdoing, which is brilliant. A lot of addicts use this atonement as a way of getting rid of their guilt and making things better, so they can stop cringing about things they have done in the past.

Of course there is nothing wrong with making up for your wrongdoing - it is to be applauded. But some addicts also see their atonement as a way of putting the past firmly behind them and not acknowledging it any more. That's all very well and has some value - but what if you could develop an even more powerful and beautiful recovery and feel happier than ever, not by ignoring your past but by *using* it? What if you could learn from your experience, acknowledge it and use it for good?

After all, what was the point of all that suffering and trauma if it hasn't done you any service or good at all? No wonder people in recovery feel like they have wasted their lives, when they haven't learnt to focus on the good things that their past has given them.

In this book I will give you the keys to making the best that you possibly can of your past, so that you can create a better future than you ever imagined. By embracing the past and actually feeling lucky that you had your addiction, you can heal from the past, feel good about yourself now and build an even more amazing future.

Don't sweep your past under the carpet and ignore it, as that means that you can never really be grateful for your recovery or celebrate your gratitude by living fully.

This is a positive book and it focuses on the positives - and if you're already thinking to yourself that there aren't really any positive things that you can say about your past, then read on. I thought the same way too, until I discovered a much better way of looking at things, and a much better way to approach my own recovery and to be truly happy.

11

I called this book *The Happy Addict* because I want to show recovering addicts that they can come to terms with their illness, their past and their present and still be happy. And that they can become addicted to happiness too. And who wouldn't want to be addicted to that?

Who this book is for

I am an alcoholic. I have used drugs during my life, but that was never my particular poison in the end. Throughout this book I will refer to the recovering person as an alcoholic, or an addict, and I will refer to alcohol and drinking more often than drugs. This book is for both alcoholics and people who have had issues with drugs, but it is a lot less clumsy to just stick to the terms relating to alcohol than to write 'alcoholic or drug addict' every single time. But whether drugs or drink was your issue, the problems encountered in recovery that we will be exploring are extremely similar, so I hope the recovering drug users will oblige me for the sake of brevity.

Additionally, this book may well be of help to people recovering from other addictions and issues, such as gambling, eating, sex addiction or compulsive spending. Again, I'm going to stick with addressing alcoholics and drug addicts specifically, but if you identify with any other addiction, forgive me for that - not all of the specific language will apply to you, but the general message certainly will.

So, to start with, I don't care how you found your recovery - whether you went 'cold turkey' with your addictive behaviour or substance of choice, whether you went to rehab, whether you attend AA, NA, CA, CODA or SMART, whether you have regular counselling or go to groups, whether you have a Higher Power or a 'God' in your life or not. My intention is not to tout any method of sobriety. I have used certain modalities and I have cemented my recovery by doing a lot of work on myself. Nothing that I mention in this book is linked to any of those recovery systems and I am not advocating any in particular. This is not about the best way to stop drinking or taking drugs, as that is a separate issue.

We all have to find our own way, the one that works best for us - and I hope that you have found yours. If you are still stuck then I would recommend reading *The Recovery Formula: An Addict's Guide to getting Clean and Sober Forever*, which is my previous book detailing the framework that you need to achieve long-term sobriety and how you can start taking steps towards recovery. But the book that you are reading right now is about how to achieve a happy, fulfilling and amazing recovery, and how to live an awesome life off the back of that.

In fact, some of you may feel that what this book has to say will clash slightly with your own particular doctrine of recovery, if you have one. Let me just reassure you that this book is designed to complement your other recovery methods. If something you are doing is keeping you clean, sober and content, then for goodness' sake, carry on doing it. But if you are not fully satisfied with your life or wonder if you could be doing anything more than you are already doing, well, that is what the book is all about.

This book is for the person who has stopped drinking or put down the drugs, but who still isn't happy with their life. Or even if you are relatively happy - I mean, we're not drinking or drugging, right? We've got to be happy that we are not stuck in the madness of using. However, if you've never looked at taking your life to any other level, other than just stopping the substances, this book will be important for you.

Maybe you've been plodding along in recovery and you're OK and fairly content, but there is room for improvement. Well this book is for you, too, as it can open your mind to new possibilities and help you see how your recovery can be even better. After all, you spent so much time having a crappy life, why not spend the rest of your time making your life amazing? It seems only fair.

Or maybe you did stop drinking, only to relapse, and you can see no good reason to go back to being sober. Did you find sobriety too difficult because you couldn't get over the past, or because you still hated yourself? Or were you bored and disappointed with your experience of recovery? This will be an extra special book for you, because it may give you that chance to go sober again, when you see how worth it sobriety and recovery really are, and how good life after addiction can be if you do certain things.

Or perhaps you're only just considering getting clean, but you think that recovery has nothing to offer you; or you're concerned that you'll be stuck in your old patterns of thinking and behaving, and you're worried that you can't change or find your way out. This book is for you, too, because it will give you hope that change is possible, and not only that, but it will show you that recovery is the place to be.

Again, I write it from the perspective of someone who is now sober and happy, because that's what I am, and that's what you can be too, whatever stage of your journey you're currently at. Recovery done properly is wonderful and amazing. Recovery done badly is painful and hard. So read on...

What does this book do?

In my Recovery Coaching service, part of my work involves helping recovering addicts to change their attitude to their experiences so that they can be even happier after their addiction than they were before it. They can appreciate their illness, rather than hating it. They can move on and become more productive and fulfilled than they could ever have been otherwise. And this is what I am going to share with you. Although it is not a substitute for personal coaching, I hope that the theories and practical exercises in this book will help you to look at recovery differently, and will make you feel ready to take your recovery to the next level.

I use a mixture of Neuro-linguistic Programming (NLP) tools, coaching techniques and modules from Dialectical Behaviour Therapy (DBT) as the backbone for my work, but a lot of what I will share with you comes from my own personal insights - having been through the journey myself and having helped others through it as well. Don't worry if you have never heard of any of the terms above - it doesn't matter. Just be prepared for some fresh thinking, some unusual new ways of looking at things and some amazing changes when you do the work.

First, let us explore some common problems that people encounter in recovery. Time and time again I hear the same issues cropping up for both recovering drug addicts and alcoholics. Being unable to let go of the past is a major one, and there are all sorts of unhelpful ways in which we may try to deal with that particular issue.

What methods have you already tried, in an attempt to get over the past? Did you merely try to think your way better? Did you just wait around for it to happen? Did you hope that time would change your feelings about the past? Did you 'fake it to make it' to no avail? Did you plod along, living on hope and promises? Did you feel over and over again the pain and frustration of not really believing you could get over the past, or draw a permanent line in the sand, or achieve something amazing? Me too!

When I first stopped drinking, I thought I was in recovery. I had put down the drink, got myself a good job, and I had gotten used to socialising and living my life without the need for a drink. But I wasn't recovered. Far from it. I was left with this awful feeling that I was a fake, that I wasn't as good as everyone else, that I wasn't 'clean' to my core.

Even when I embarked upon long-term sobriety, I was so desperately unhappy that I sought counselling after work, just to have someone to tell my terrible troubles to. My counsellor was a lovely woman, who wanted so badly to help me. She told me how proud I should be of being sober and how strong I was, but I just wasn't buying it.

I remember every week, on a Wednesday evening after work, telling my counsellor the same thing - "I just can't get over the past. I just don't *feel* recovered." It felt so frustrating, as I was not drinking and was living a respectable and fairly enjoyable life overall. But inside, I felt like I was a fake, and it was tearing me up. Do you know what she told me, and what you may yourself have been told? It takes time and patience.

Well that's all very well, but I couldn't wait and in the end I relapsed - big time. You see, despite the outward trappings of recovery, I hadn't really believed that I was better; and I wasn't.

I had been 'white-knuckling it' every day because of my own mind-set. No matter how badly I wanted to be recovered, I just couldn't believe in myself, because I remained stuck in my old way of thinking. To the outside world, I looked like I was walking the walk, but inside I was dragging myself along by my fingernails, still desperately lost.

And when I eventually relapsed, no matter how much I desperately tried to stay sober, I just couldn't. I had lost faith in myself entirely. Any small amount of faith that I'd ever had was utterly gone. From time to time, I would pick myself up and feel strong, and I'd tell myself I was going to beat it; but I couldn't even last a month sober. The longest sobriety I had in my whole nightmare relapse was just under 30 days - and that was on Antabuse, the medication that hospitalises you if you decide to drink on it. Even a proverbial gun to my head couldn't stop me drinking.

Bruised and battered as I was, the one valuable thing that I learned from that whole extended relapse was that there had to be another way. I had to learn to do things differently from the way I had been doing them before. And so, I set out to find the keys to unlock the door to a solid and happy recovery, which I had been missing all along.

I did a lot of research, put myself through a lot of trial and error, and had a series of epiphanies, before I realised that I needed to look at changing my entire way of thinking about my experiences or I would never be free. And one major step for me was to start to actually *appreciate* them for what they had given me, instead of regretting them. That really was a big turning point - looking at my past as a positive, and not a negative.

When I started implementing my new plan and looked at how I could use my experiences effectively to actually *help* myself, things finally started changing. And from that space, I was able to add in all sorts of other tools to cement my recovery and finally start to bloom and celebrate the gift that recovery is.

In this book, I will share with you what took me from being the Relapse Queen to someone who is now very proud of my recovery. Someone who is now an author, an entrepreneur, and a massive proponent of recovery. Someone who is not ashamed to tell my story, nor to show my scars. And more importantly, I am someone who can now help others to escape from the same trap that I fell into. That is the most important part of all. And I hope that I can help you, too.

Format

This book consists of fifteen chapters, each one devoted to one of the keys that you will need to unlock the door to the ultimate recovery. Each of these keys will be a vital part of the approach you need to take in order to achieve the same thing as I and my clients have. What I can give you are the tools to work towards a peace of mind unequalled in people who sideline their addiction, who sweep it sneakily under the carpet in an attempt to move on.

And this book will enable you to use your new-found qualities and resources; to become comfortable with yourself, to be happy and proud. At the end of each section, you'll get a coaching session, in which I will give you a couple of exercises to complete to ensure that the knowledge you have gained from the previous chapter has sunk in - and that you are committed to taking action on it. These are very practical exercises and I strongly recommend that you take the time to do them. After all, I am sure you believe your recovery is worth a bit of effort. There will also be a short summary of key points at the end of each chapter, for easy reference when you return to the book, along with an appropriate quotation or two to illustrate one of the main messages of each chapter.

The first time that you read this book, please read it in order, from beginning to end, and do the exercises. If you want to go back over the chapters again, then of course feel free to do so, and you can read it as many times as you want. There may be certain parts you will want to go back to in times of trouble, and most of the exercises are designed to be done multiple times.

But the very first time you read this book, go with the flow and read the chapters in the order in which they are written. It has been written so that it makes most sense in this order. I hope you will enjoy sharing my personal journey as you read the book, and follow your own.

Chapter One

Do you Happen to be Best Friends with Doctor Who?

Have you got a time machine? Or do you count Doctor Who as one of your best mates? Has he promised to lend you his Tardis any time you want? Or maybe you're Sam Beckett? No, not the writer. You know, that guy out of Quantum Leap. The one who travels back and forth in time and space, taking over the minds of different people to try to change their lives for them. You're not a fan of 70s TV? Never mind. My point is that only fictional characters can become somebody else for the day, or travel back in time to change the past. You can't.

OK, so that's obvious, right? I'm sure you know that intellectually. If it's so obvious, then why are you constantly harking back to the past, getting stuck in the things that happened to you, or feeling guilty about the things you did to others? Bless you. I did it too, trying to do the impossible. I seemed to believe that if I wished hard enough, then I could be somebody else or I could alter the course of history. But I couldn't.

Now just because you can not change the past in physical terms of what you did, or what happened to you, it doesn't mean you can't change your reaction to the past or your way of thinking about it.

In this book we are going to be looking at the past, but not in the negative or wishful way that you might be used to. We are not going to regret anything, nor sit around mourning our misfortunes, nor playing the 'If only...' game. We can use the past for practical purposes, but not as a feeding-ground for fantasy or regret. The past is over. You can not change it, so you are wasting your time wishing you could.

Another crime I was guilty of was believing that just because I'd had an awful past, it made me a bad person, a person who couldn't get things right, a person who had some deep, murky soul that would never be redeemed. Utter rubbish. My life now shows that I can operate up there with the best of them. There is no '*Rocky* moment' for me. There is no "I could've been a contender..." speech; because I *am* a contender. Even though I wasn't always, thank goodness I finally pulled myself out of my difficulties, and I am now.

But there was a time when that wasn't the case at all. There was a point in my life where I believed that it was all too late and that I had been through too much to really make a spectacular life for myself. In fact, there was a point where I didn't see much of a life for myself at all. A point at which I was completely held back by the past and a sense of my own limitations.

The first time I got sober, I was eager to undo all the damage that I had done to others in the course of my addiction. As soon as I thought I was getting well, I started trying to atone for the past. I apologised to my friends and family, I spent quality 'make-up' time with people, I bought presents, I made grand gestures and I generally started being Mrs Nice Gal. But underneath all of it, I couldn't forgive myself, no matter what I did.

My loved ones would sometimes get quite exasperated with me - because they had forgiven me and wanted me to be happy. My own mother, who had for years put up with my moods, my drunken sobbing phone calls, my abusive language, the worry of not knowing how I was doing, who I was with, what was happening to me, or if I would drop dead at any time, told me not to be so hard on myself. I was doing all the right things now - and that was all that mattered to her. But that wasn't enough for me - no, I had to go on self-flagellating, hating myself, and everything I had done.

I kept trying to trace it back to a cause, so that I might be able to lay the blame at someone else's door. Maybe it all went wrong because of something that happened to me when I was young; maybe that one long illness I had as a youngster sent me down the wrong road; maybe I had hung out with the wrong people; maybe I was just too damn sensitive for this world after all and should never have been born. I used to be a bit of a dramatic sort, me, given half a chance.

I think the most difficult thought-trap that I got stuck in was that I never believed I would ever truly be redeemed of what had happened - and that was because, outside of the bubble of intoxication, I now realised my mortality. I only had one life, and a lot of it was already gone. I felt like so much of my life had been wasted, utterly wasted, gone down the drain; time I could never reclaim. And that kept me miserable. The more I thought about it, the more horribly depressed I became. My catchphrase was "It'll *never* be alright *ever* again." Yeah, I told you I was dramatic.

That genuinely was my catchphrase throughout my drinking years, and I even repeated it for a long time when I was sober. During the chaos of my drinking, I had been in some bad places, physically and mentally, and I had felt some terribly painful feelings. I took seven overdoses, ended up in two mental hospitals, got raped twice, had an abortion and worked as a semi-prostitute just for somewhere to live. And that's the edited version. It was a horrible existence and I used to have the Samaritans on speed-dial.

My mind was scarred; my body is still scarred. And so I carried my woeful catchphrase into sobriety. I had lost my innocence and would never get it back - and so I would never be 'clean'.

That dreadful waste of my twenties plagued me - when everyone else was out and about, having fun and being young and full of life, I was mostly ill or moving from one crazy situation to the next. When all my peers were graduating from university, creating careers or starting families, I thought my life was already over.

And when I did stop drinking, all those people were already way ahead of me. They had enjoyed themselves and built up good lives for nearly a decade, while I was in and out of hospital, and I was left with nothing to show for all that time. "Those should have been the best years of my life," I thought, "and they're all gone."

Now you can see how I came to that conclusion, and many of you may have come to adopt the same sort of fatalistic mantra, even if you never verbalised it in the same way that I did. Even if you've never laid it out in those black and white terms before, you may know exactly what it means to be stuck in the past, no matter how much you try to move on.

Well, this is where I came to a shocking realisation. What if all I was doing by worrying about the past, cursing myself and hating everything I had ever done before, was simply wasting more time? There may have been a part of me that was hating myself in order to punish myself for the awful things I'd done, or the people I had hurt. And that was a good-hearted part of me - but that part had all the wrong ideas.

If I genuinely felt bad about the things that I had done, wasn't it more productive to do amazing things with my future? What if I could make my family happier than they'd ever been and prouder of me than they ever could have dreamed possible? Wasn't that the way to make it up to them? And wasn't that a way that would make both them, and me, happy?

And as for that part of me which was worried about all the time I had wasted - well wasn't I wasting even more time now, when I'd been given this amazing gift of sobriety? Was I going to celebrate that and honour it by clinging onto things I couldn't change? Hell, no.

The day I realised how unhelpful it was to me, and to anyone else with whom I came into contact, for me to be hanging onto my past like a ball and chain was the day I decided to stop it. It sounds so simple, and actually, that's because it is. The first step in making an amazing recovery is to just decide that you are going to stop focussing on the past in a negative way. No man, woman, child, nor Doctor Who himself, can change your past - but you *can* change the present, and by doing that, you can determine the future.

For those of you who are still struggling with the concept of it being an easy decision to make, read this chapter over again and come back to this place in the book. Do it now. Go on...

Did you do it? Are you back? Oh, look. You've just wasted more time. Do you want to go back and read it again? Do you *get it* now? It's pointless, useless and counterproductive to carry on holding onto the past. It doesn't serve you, your loved ones, your friends or family; it doesn't serve your employers, your children or anyone you will have in your life from now on. Stop wasting more time, when you could be becoming a better person and building an incredible life instead.

There will be more on the past later in the book - but we won't be dwelling on it this time. We'll be using it for good! If you are finding it hard to imagine getting unstuck from it, there will be more on this later on to help you. In the meantime, it's time to complete your first coaching exercise. Give it a go - there's no time like the present.

Exercises:

Minimising 'Magic'

This is a very powerful exercise and it's very easy to do. Some of you may have read the last chapter with a sort of disbelief. As if what I have said is easy to understand intellectually, but difficult to do. You may not imagine it is that easy to get over some of the more traumatic things that may have happened to you during your past, or to just forget about certain painful memories in order to move forward.

If you find that one incident or another from the past is 'haunting' you, we're just going to take the impact out of it with this exercise. Do not use this exercise on anything horribly traumatic - you would need to work with a qualified NLP Practitioner or therapist to work on any problems of that sort.

But think of something that has irritated or annoyed you or something you can't quite get over. Maybe it was a cutting remark from a colleague or something a friend did that made you hurt and upset. Something that still stings a little. Got one?

Right, now most of us create a picture of our memories in our minds, so make sure you've got the picture of that incident in your head right now. And then I want you to turn that picture black and white. If you find it difficult to just snap the picture into a different colour, then imagine your picture on an old TV set that has a dial to change the colour - and see yourself just turning that colour down so it all drains slowly away into black and white.

Next, I want you to make that picture smaller. So just shrink the picture down, from however big it is in your mind, into the size of a postage stamp. You can even make the picture blurry, fuzzy or remove any sounds you might associate with it.

Noticed anything? Yeah, I'll bet you aren't feeling as upset or worried about that incident now. This exercise will work for the vast majority of people with any experience that is moderately upsetting. You can use it on anything of that calibre that you'd like to. I hope it will also show you that from now on you don't have to think about things in the same way that you always have. That is the point of this book - to show you a better way.

The Present Tense

I call this exercise 'The Present Tense', firstly because it is about focussing on the here and now, and secondly because when you first try it, you may find it is uncomfortable and quite difficult (yeah, tense). Read the instructions through completely first - and then try it out for yourself.

So, I just want you to start off by relaxing completely and thinking of where you are right now. Whether you're in the bedroom, the lounge or wherever you are, just be still and focus on the 'now'. Focus on you, sitting there, breathing and present. For three minutes I want you to think of nothing but the present time and focus your attention on your breath going in and out of your body.

The idea is to not allow your mind wander into the future, or back into the past, but to mentally stay with where you are right this instant.

Of course, this is almost impossible the first time you do it. You'll start thinking of all sorts of things, such as "What am I having for dinner?" "What about that errand I have to run?" "Did I tell my other half what time to be home?" "How will I know when my three minutes is up?" That's OK and it's completely normal - just gently pull your mind back to your breathing again whenever you find it 'wandering away' from the present moment.

Resist the urge to 'tell yourself off' for letting your mind wander. Just pull your attention back to the present, without judgement and without criticism. Let go of any thoughts other than those involving where you are right now in the present.

OK that's all of the instructions. Do the exercise for three minutes and then come back to this place in the book.

When you have done the exercise, what did that teach you? I hope that you have become aware of all the time you are spending time-travelling, going back into the past or forward into the future, thinking about things other than what is going on in the present moment. Don't worry about it; don't criticise yourself. We all do it. The purpose is to be aware of it.

The reason I want you to become aware of it, is that the more time you spend pointlessly focussing on the past or the future, the less time you have in the present. And the present moment is all we have.

There is nothing you can do right this moment to change anything in the past, or alter anything in the future. So it is infinitely better to focus on what is happening right now. It is only when you realise how much time-travelling you truly do, that you can make a conscious effort to lessen the amount of time you spend doing it.

The more you do this exercise, the easier it will become to actually pull your mind back to your breathing and the here-and-now.

Try doing it once a day for a few minutes until you find it easier to be in the present. Doing this exercise in the longer term has all sorts of additional benefits - it will make you calmer, more peaceful, and better able to deal with your emotions.

Take-aways:

- Don't let yourself get held back by the past
- You can not change the past
- You can not be someone else
- You only have power over the present moment
- Stop wasting time and start to create an amazing life now

"Although no-one can go back and make
a brand new start, anyone can start from now
and make a brand new ending"

- Carl Bard

"The past is a ghost, the future a dream,
and all we ever have is now."

- Bill Cosby

Chapter Two

Life's a Bitch and then you Try

I mentioned blame very briefly in the last chapter, and for good reason. If for some reason you haven't already left the past behind, it may be because you are still trapped in the blame game. And I don't blame you for that, ironically, as I did that too. I was the most self-pitying alcoholic around when I was drinking. And quite frankly, I had every right to be, too.

I started my all-day every-day drinking pattern at the age of eighteen, after I had developed symptoms of what I now know is called Social Phobia, or Social Anxiety Disorder. Now for years I had no idea that I suffered from a disorder or what that meant - all I knew that was I found life terrifying. I only found out later that my collective symptoms had a name and were diagnosable as a condition.

My symptoms started just as I was leaving secondary school and going on to Sixth Form College. Among the first symptoms that I developed was a fear of people watching me eat lunch. I was always worried that they would make some sort of judgement about what I was eating, that I was eating too much or too little, or the wrong type of food. So I either wouldn't eat at all or I would go and eat my sandwiches in a toilet cubicle where no-one could see me. Disgusting I know, but that reflects just how much I couldn't bear people to see me eating.

The next thing that happened was that I became scared of walking home alone. At college, my classes finished early on a Tuesday - and instead of walking for half an hour to get home, I'd hang around all day in the common room so I could get a lift with a friend when everyone else had finished their classes. I felt a strange and terrifying sensation whenever I dared to walk home - I'd be very conscious of people watching me walking, and I worried that they'd make judgements about my clothes or how I looked - or even how I was walking! I would sometimes put really loud music on my walkman to distract me, but it didn't work very well, and if my batteries ran out when I was halfway home, I'd be in sheer panic. And so I rarely went anywhere on my own in those days if I could avoid it.

I just thought I was agoraphobic, which would have been bad enough, but all the rest of the symptoms of Social Phobia made it nigh on impossible to function as a normal human being. I was scared of everything! Shopping, walking, eating, people looking at me, people talking about me, putting forward my own opinions, stating my preferences or saying what I did or didn't like. I was so caught up in the fear that I tried to self-medicate by drinking alcohol.

And the more I drank alcohol to dull that fear, the more I realised what a wonderful antidote it was. So by the age of eighteen, I was already an alcoholic, and by the age of nineteen I had become fully dependent and drank all day, every day. By the time I went off to university, I had taken to carrying a little bottle of Sprite round with me everywhere I went, which I would dutifully fill with gin every morning, adding a dash of lemonade to disguise the smell a bit. And that would get me through the day's classes until I could go home, hide away and continue drinking freely on my own.

I called it 'living in my bubble', the only way I could function. I didn't really socialise with the other students much at university. While everyone else was meeting new people, making lifelong friendships and enjoying being young and free, I shacked up with a drug dealer and survived on gin and occasional biscuits. And so started my chaotic and miserable life as an addict.

For a long time, I didn't want to stop drinking. I knew I was an alcoholic and I wasn't interested in stopping because I knew how terrifying life was for me without a protective, hazy shield.

And of course, I was the biggest self-pitier going, especially as the years went by and my life became even more insane and unhealthy. And actually, I am not saying I didn't have good reason to be sad and bitter. I think that every one of you who has ended up as an addict or alcoholic has a right to pity yourself in the first instance.

I believe that everyone who had an awful childhood, or a traumatic past, has a right to feel that they've been dealt a rough hand in life. I think everyone who suffers from depression, anxiety disorders or personality disorders, and everyone who has been so abused and mistreated in their lives that it has driven them to drink or take drugs, has an absolute right to feel pissed off and fed up. People who are bewildered by their inability to moderate their substance use or their behaviour have the right to rue their condition.

It's *not* fair that all these awful things have happened to us. It's not fair and it's not right. But here's my question: Are you going to carry on pitying yourself, or are you going to decide to change your life?

While we are not responsible for the crummy upbringings, the damaging people, the psychological difficulties, the genes, the problems, the feelings and situations that we may have been handed in life, we are the *only* people that can do something about NOW.

If this world is really so unfair that it's given you all this hardship to deal with, do you really think it's going to take it all away as well? It's not - and all the self-pity in the world will not make a damn bit of difference to that.

When I was finally trying to actually stop my alcoholic drinking, I would find myself drawn time and time again to the old routine of "Why me? Why do I have to go through all this stuff?" I believed I was a nice person, and I didn't understand why I had to struggle when so many other people were living their normal lives around me, without half the problems I had.

And I was right; it wasn't fair and there wasn't necessarily any rhyme or reason as to why those things had happened to me. But, I could either sit there endlessly complaining and remain stuck in this pitiful life I had, paralysed by my awful problems - or I could change it and become a better, happier person.

There is no choice to make, really, when you put it like that. And yet sometimes I was still drawn back into the old self-pity; until I really started to see clearly, that while I am *not* responsible for having my problems, I *am* responsible for my life and how it pans out. While some kooky film-maker might have given me an awful script with some traumatic scenes, and a whole plethora of obstacles, it was up to me to make the final cut and ensure the protagonist won through in the end.

That's it - simple but life-changing. I have to be responsible for turning my own life around. It's not something I was particularly happy to have handed to me - I would've much preferred not to have to do it at all. But I realised that it was the only way that I was ever likely to be happy - by accepting responsibility for my own life and my own attitude. Maybe not in the past, but right NOW. After all, what was the alternative? It was to continue my horrible, cruddy life until I died a miserable, alcoholic mess. And I wasn't having that. And neither should you.

Do you realise that you actually owe it to yourself to make your life better? If it's been utterly rubbish so far, then really no-one could blame you for wanting the rest of it to be super-fantastic with bells on. It kind of evens it out, doesn't it? And that requires work. You may have more work to do than some people who have had less to contend with, but I guarantee that you'll feel a sense of pride so much bigger than they do when you start achieving. You know how you always root for the underdog? Well, start rooting for *you*.

You don't get a second chance at life when it's over. It's too late when you're dead. But luckily, you can give yourself a second chance at life when you're in recovery. And if you do it properly, you can end up in a better place than you ever imagined.

I know that when I was looking out from under the all-encompassing, self-pity-filled duvet of despair (a figurative one, mainly - I'm sure you had one too) at the people who had survived adversity and gone on to achieve amazing things, I'd sigh sadly, wish I was them and wonder how they did it.

And then I realised, that's it. They *did* it. They didn't wish for it, they didn't label themselves as people who couldn't do it because of their harsh hand in life. They didn't look at other people in wonder and admiration and then settle back down to cry for a bit. They decided to take responsibility for making their life awesome. And they *did* it.

That's the only difference between the winners and losers in life - the winners are the ones who decide to take responsibility, who commit to working hard and taking action. It doesn't matter how far back you have come from, as long as you are committed to making yourself a winner in the end. It's not about where you start, but where you finish. And you're allowed to cut yourself some slack, to make mistakes, and to cry when you're upset. But have the end in mind at all times - you are a person who is going to *make* it. You are - and I know you are, because you're reading this book.

Your responsibility for your life and your future is not just one all-encompassing task either. It breaks down into a myriad of little things that you can take responsibility for; like taking responsibility for your mood and for your happiness. For some of us, it may be difficult to believe that no-one can make us unhappy except ourselves. But we might just be able to believe that we can take responsibility for *un*-making ourselves unhappy. I don't think it is particularly helpful when we are hurt or upset about things for people to say to us:

"Just deal with it. Pull your socks up!" But I do think it is useful for us to know that we can either let ourselves continue to be upset or we can responsibly say "No, I'm not having this," and sort ourselves out from there on in. The first time you manage to *un*-make yourself upset is quite a revelation, as you realise the power you have over your moods, and how you let people affect you.

Now I hope no-one thinks my tone is harsh here. As I said, I do not blame you for feeling more than a little cheesed off about the situation you may have found yourself in. But I do need to impress upon you the reality of the situation. It was only when I woke up and realised that no-one else could change my life except me, that I started getting serious about taking responsibility for myself.

And do you know what? Responsibility isn't some terrible great burden as some of you may think it is. It's a wonderfully freeing thing to know that you can be in charge of your destiny rather than just 'have things happen to you'. Being responsible gives you self-respect, independence, purpose and, above all, freedom. And who wouldn't want that?

Exercises

The Reckless Decision-Maker

If you read the last chapter with a certain ambivalence, it might be because you believe that you have never been able to be responsible for anything ever in your life. "Come on, Beth. You're talking to alkies and junkies here! We're reckless! Who's more irresponsible than us?!" Granted, I hear this a lot from people who have lived chaotic lives of addiction. They believe they have never ever been responsible for anything. But actually that just isn't true. In order to get the idea out of your mind that you're not able to be responsible, and never have been, we're going to look at your life. Have you ever made a decision in your life? Yes? Then you have been responsible for making that decision. No matter how reckless your decisions have been, the fact that you have made them means that you took responsibility upon yourself for making that decision.

Now let's look at some more concrete and even more responsible examples. Have you ever met a deadline? Have you ever held a position? Have you ever been trusted with a secret or with a pet? This can go right back to your school days. Did you have a task at school that you were responsible for, like being a milk monitor or a dinner server or putting chairs away? Did you ever belong to any clubs where you took on certain tasks? Have you ever been part of a team?

If your parents were working, or otherwise engaged, were you responsible for making yourself breakfast or getting yourself off to school?

When you first started living on your own, were you responsible for shopping, cooking or cleaning? Have you ever been responsible for making someone else's meals or paying bills or filling in forms? For changing utility suppliers or for collecting money?

Now, if you considered things that you were supposed to be responsible for during your active addiction, you may argue that many times you let others down and did not treat your responsibilities properly - of course it was difficult during that turbulent time to do that, but don't worry about it. You will still be able to find times when you *were* responsible and completed your tasks if you think about it.

I would like you to make a list of 25 things you have been responsible for in your life, no matter how far back they were, or how trivial they seem now. At the time, they were important responsibilities. Use examples from any time in your life when you had responsibilities. It's important that you do this exercise before you move onto the next one. If you think you can't come up with 25, then just write out the numbers 1-25, fill out as many of the numbers as you can and go back to it later. You will find you can fill out the entire list in the end.

The Guard Dog

If taking responsibility feels new to you, we're going to ease you into it by exploring how it feels to be really responsible.

Can you imagine how responsible a guard dog must feel? If a guard dog was thinking about his job, you would think he'd feel pretty responsible about it, wouldn't you?

Now this exercise may seem a little strange, but it's scientific, I promise you. I'd like you to imagine that you are a guard dog. Yes, you read that right. You don't have to start barking or wagging your imaginary tail or anything like that (unless that floats your boat), but I'd like you to get into the mind of a guard dog.

If you were supposed to be protecting a baby asleep in a cradle, and you were stationed at the door of the sleeping child's bedroom, just imagine what that would be like. Take some time to get into the guard dog's mind-set. Don't just think about the emotions he might be feeling, but really get into them and imagine actually feeling them. See through the eyes of the dog.

What would you, as a guard dog, protecting a sleeping baby, feel like? Would you feel proud? Protective? Alert? Trusted? What else might you feel like? Really feel those feelings. This is important.

If you really feel too weird about pretending to be a dog then you can use a person - choose someone very responsible though! I usually prefer people to be a dog, because guard dogs tend not to waver in their tenacity and commitment to the task. If you want, you could choose a marine, or a nanny or anyone else who has to be very responsible for something precious. And really feel those feelings.

And once you've experienced those feelings, take them and just translate them across to your own life. What do you feel like now when you think about taking responsibility for your life? Doesn't it feel nice to be the guard dog for your own life?

Take-aways:

- Life is not fair, but we can work to make it fairer
- You are the only person who can change things in your life
- You are responsible for your life now
- Taking responsibility for yourself is liberating

"Success on any major scale requires you to accept responsibility... In the final analysis, the one quality that all successful people have is the ability to take on responsibility."

- Michael Korda

Chapter Three

The Magical Sobriety Fairy

What do you mean you've never heard of the magical sobriety fairy? She must exist, right? After all, I see a lot of recovering addicts just hanging around waiting for her to pop into their lives and make everything wonderful.

Time and time again, people who are newly clean and sober tell me that they are bored, or that life is no better at the moment. Some recovering addicts even have moments when they wish they were still drinking or drugging, because at least life was exciting and full of drama back then.

It is normal to go through a period of feeling a bit low when you put down the drink or the drugs. You are likely to feel flat or bored for a while. And this is due to a few different factors at play.

Firstly, your brain has undergone chemical changes as a result of your addiction. It is not going to go back to normal overnight. Additionally, when you are using drink and drugs, you are more likely to feel massive emotional swings, as you experience the elation or buzz of using, and then the drinkers' blues, and the low of the hangover or comedown. Normal, everyday emotions can feel quite flat and boring when compared to the roller-coaster you were on.

In the same way, people who are coming out of an addictive behaviour will usually have encountered damage and chaos, which although negative, was also exciting and exhilarating. Getting up each day and facing the realities of jam and toast in the morning rather than carnage and dread may feel flat in comparison, even if it is much better in reality.

Not only that, but psychologically too, you're going to feel different - many people feel like they don't fit in any more, when everyone else around them seems to be drinking or doing drugs and they're not. It has become so ingrained in our culture that you must drink to have fun that people who don't drink are seen as abnormal. It's an awful thing that has come to pass here, but it is reality. You may feel like a misfit, like you will never again have the chance to do some of the fun and crazy stuff you used to do - and that can be depressing and bring you down. Similarly, it is easy to feel isolated if you have had to leave behind certain people and places when you quit using.

If you're fairly new to sobriety, you may even find that you feel rather sad, lost and confused. Yep, I've been there too. Most people are absolutely baffled by who they are and what they should be doing in life when they first stop drinking or drugging. I remember the first time I ever put down the drink for more than three consecutive weeks, I was absolutely lost and I didn't know whether I was coming or going. I had lived my life in the cloud of intoxication for so long, that I didn't really know who I was and it was very daunting to think about finding out.

I remember very clearly that I questioned all sorts of things. At the time I was living in North London with my boyfriend. We had a house together and at the time I was an aspiring Journalist. And when I put down the drink, I was plagued by this horrible feeling of not knowing who I was.

As I emerged from the haze, I started to think that my life was all wrong, and that I should probably be a lesbian writer living in Paris. That was based on a long-held dream of living in France and the fact that I was questioning my relationship at the time, as I had been rushed into a commitment. Newly sober, I was fairly reactionary and pretty lost overall.

I wrote the following paragraphs in my journal at two months sober:

"All of a sudden now the clouds of alcohol haze have lifted, I find myself not knowing who I am and stuck in a life where I can't find out what I am.

"Because I have travelled through the past ten years of my life in a haze, my thoughts and feelings have never had a chance to emerge like this before. I feel like I have 'ended up' with life where I am now, and it is not really something I have actively chosen. I have started feeling so unsure of who I am, and uncertain of not only what I want, but what I need in life.

"It sounds like it should be a lovely feeling, knowing that I can now do so many things that I just couldn't when my drinking was out of control. So many more opportunities. But it's not; it's horrible. I feel like I have lost all sense of who I am and have wasted so many years maybe living the wrong life. Thinking about this, I feel like a huge, hot claw is tearing at my insides and I just want it to stop."

Blimey, I was in a sorry place wasn't I? A lot of recovering addicts expect that life will immediately just start to get better once they've stopped taking their poison of choice. After all, they're doing the right thing, so life should reward them, right?

I wish that life was like that. I often wonder at the way nature works. Why is it that you sometimes have to suffer agonising withdrawals when you're doing the right thing by *stopping* drinking or taking drugs? Why is it that smokers, for example, can have a 20-a-day habit, and then they start to get ill and cough up all sorts of weird stuff when they chuck away the ciggies? It's odd isn't it? You would think nature would reward us for doing the right, healthy and sane thing. But it doesn't work like that initially, and this is another of those 'Ah, such is life' moments that we just have to accept. The world is full of contradictions, paradoxes and conundrums - and this is just another of those.

So, what can we do in this instance? Number one, just accept that you are going to feel a little less chirpy than you might have imagined when newly sober. Some people do experience the 'Pink Cloud' of sobriety early on and others don't even have that. But either way, the Pink Cloud is so called for a reason - it floats away on the wind after a short period of time.

While you might be fortunate enough to get encouragement from your peers, friends or family for putting down the drink or drugs, sadly the Magical Sobriety Fairy isn't going to come down from anywhere and hand you an award, a ton of cash and the most beautiful person on the planet to share it with. If you want a new life, you have to go out there and create it.

While some may find this disheartening (after all you've done a load of work *already* haven't you?!) actually if you think about it in the correct way, it's utterly inspiring. Please see above for a great example of someone who wasn't thinking about it in the correct way the very first time she got sober. (Me, in case any of you have forgotten already.)

You now have the power to create any life you want - with anything and anyone you want in it. You finally get to create the life of your dreams - and nothing that's worth having comes easy. The very fact that you will have to work for it means that you will be happier and prouder of this cool, new life that you've created. And it's all crafted from your unique blueprint of what you want. I think that's pretty amazing. That's enough to put the spring back into your step isn't it? Hmm, well at least you're thinking about it.

This is what I find so powerful in my coaching business - the people I see have the opportunity to become who they were always *meant* to be. It's like being a brand new person with a whole life ahead that can be as fantastic as you want - if you're prepared to take the steps to do it. Dreams which are not acted on are the saddest things of all. If you want to dream without taking action you may as well stay in bed. As sad as it is to say, many a relapse has been caused by the feeling of boredom or ennui. Well, if you weren't convinced by my 'happy-clappy' reason for getting on with it before, hopefully you will be by that one.

Contrary to public perception, there are only a few ingredients that are needed for success. They just need to be done consistently. And the most important thing of all is taking action. I know some of you will only be comfortable with 'baby steps' at first - and that's alright, as long as you are making progress.

Once you've seen how far a few baby steps can take you, then I hope you'll grow in confidence and be inspired by all sorts of things happening that will make you want to just keep on taking action and taking bigger and bigger strides. Just because you want to walk before you can run, if you feel safer that way, it doesn't mean you shouldn't canter along once you've started tasting success and have realised that you can achieve anything you set your mind to.

While we're on the subject of baby steps, I'm only going to allow those of you who really feel that it is your best interest to take them to do so - *not* those of you who are arguing for your limitations!

If you have to take baby steps to keep yourself safe, if you're very newly clean and sober and know that stresses would put you at risk, then crawl if you have to as long as you're making progress. But for those of you who just *believe* it should be baby steps because that's what addicts are supposed to do, I'm not having you holding yourself back in that way.

It's an understandable reaction in recovery to want to get on with things quietly and hide ourselves away a bit - because addiction is seen to be a shameful illness. Currently society, for the most part, deems us to be some of the lowest creatures on Earth - especially the poor junkies. I hope that the recent drive to promote recovery and celebrate it will change that in time - it will if I have anything to do with it! But because of the way that we have been looked at for so long, we feel so caught up in our own stigmatisation that we feel we are not worthy of playing big.

Our guilt is so great from our past that we always feel limited. We think we are massive failures in life - but we're not at all! We're people that became ill, and if you're reading this book and are in recovery, I hope you can start to see that you're a winner! And if you're not yet in recovery and are thinking about signing up to the clean and sober brigade, I hope you take heart in knowing that you will be among the winners, too.

One of the reasons that I took so long to ask for the correct kind of help for my own addiction, was that I felt guilty about struggling with my sobriety. It was embarrassing enough being an addict, because of the way people view the issue, but additionally, I felt that I was somehow weak if I couldn't beat my problems on my own. I believed that I should be strong enough to be able to sort my own illness out, especially since some of my initial reasons for turning to the bottle were no longer current.

Out of sheer desperation, following a serious incident, and the fear of coming to a very sticky end indeed more quickly than I had imagined, I finally did ask for help. And while I hated doing that and it took me a while to change my mind-set, I did finally come to realise that I was a stronger person for asking for help. I saw that it was courageous to admit that I had a problem that was too big for me alone to handle. Weak people hide; strong people stand up and ask for help.

If you needed to have a heart bypass, you would be called stupid and foolhardy if you bought a do-it-yourself scalpel kit and tried to attempt it on your own. It would be entirely appropriate to contact an expert to get them to help you out. And it's the same with this illness. We don't 'give up' and ask for help; we give *over* and ask for help, because it is the only sane and strong thing to do. And it's still a long, hard fight sometimes, even with others' help. But it's still a hell of a lot easier and nicer than doing it on your own.

And so anyone that suffers from an addiction disorder and is still feeling guilty and ashamed, or afraid of asking for extra support, should ask themselves, why should I be ashamed of being ill? And why should I be ashamed of myself as a recovering addict? Why shouldn't I celebrate my progress, even if I sometimes have setbacks? I don't blame you for feeling bad about your illness, because, after all, it comes from the society around us. But if you look at it from a logical perspective and put it down on paper in black and white, you will see that it is society's thinking that is faulty here. We are successes, not failures.

I don't know about you, but I'm not going to let an antiquated opinion of society's, based on a lack of understanding, anger and fear, stop me from seeing things as they really are. I'm not going to let that stop me living my life and I'm not going to feel ashamed of my illness for one minute more. I'm not going to play small because of my past. I have just as much right to enjoy the rewards of life as the next person. And I have just as much right to stand up and be proud of myself and my life as anyone else. Especially now that I am in recovery and contributing positively to society.

The following exercises illustrate very nicely what I should have done when I was writing out that journal entry, feeling alone and lost. The first step everyone should take when they need to find out who they are, is to look at their values, because living according to your values is what makes you happiest in life. If you start pulling away from them, that is when you become really unhappy and discontent.

Your values are the starting place for all your beliefs, actions and behaviours. Your values may have become obscured during your drinking or drugging. In fact one of the reasons why you became so unhappy during that time is probably because you were living in a way that really didn't correspond with your values or how you wanted to live. Unless you value being trapped, frustrated and sad, then I guess you were not living according to your values at all.

So, do the first exercise below to find out what your values really are - whether this is a reclamation of them or the first time you have ever looked at them. And once, you've found out your values, it is much easier to find out what you want to do, and be, in life.

Exercises

What 'Matters' Matters!

There are a few ways of finding out your values and what really matters to you in life. I could just give you a list and ask you to circle your values, but sometimes this doesn't unearth the real results.

Sometimes when people do this, they circle what they think other people would *want* them to say. So we are going to go a little deeper and ask some questions to discover what your real values are. So, answer the questions below honestly - remember no-one needs to see this except you. It is important that you get to your true values, because following them and living them is the very foundation of what will make you happy in life. Now, get a pen and paper and answer the following questions. Take as long as you need to find meaningful answers.

1. Who are your heroes?

    Think about two or three people you admire. It doesn't matter if they are celebrities or people close to you. They do not necessarily have to have achieved anything astonishing, but can just be people whom you really respect and admire.

2. What do you enjoy doing?

Choose three or four things that you really enjoy. I don't mean things you do just to pass the time, or things that you do because your friends like doing them, but activities that you really, really like doing, whether you do them once a year or once a day.

3. When was a really happy time in your life?

Think about a specific event if you can, or if not, then a period of time will do. Pick a few examples if you can. If you genuinely can not think of any happy times in your life, then instead, write down things that you believe would make you really happy.

4. When have you felt most fulfilled?

What were you doing? Again, choosing a specific event is helpful, but a certain period of your life, or an activity that brings out this feeling of fulfilment, is fine too.

Now that you have answered the questions, we are going to use those answers to draw out your values. If you become stuck at any time with actually identifying the values that are important to you, I have provided a list of values at the back of this book. But try to go with your gut instinct here, as those answers will most likely be the right ones.

For the answer to the first question, ask yourself what is it about these people you admire? You may have to drill down through a few levels to get there. For example, one of my heroes is someone you will never have heard of, so let's just call him Mr X.

Mr X was an ex-addict and a professional I once worked with and what I admired about him was that he had stopped drinking, among other things. But while I admired that he had stopped drinking, that did not give me the values that I admired, so I had to go down a little further to discover the values underlying this that I most appreciated. So, they were values like Courage, Resilience, Strength and Peace.

And now onto the second question. Again, drill down and find the values underlying what you really love doing. For example, I really love volunteering to help the homeless over Christmas, and what I love about that is Giving and Helping Others. But another thing I like about doing it is that I am doing something different from everyone else. So some of my values surrounding that might be Individuality or Rule-Breaking as well.

For the third question, you should have identified some really happy times in your life or things that would make you happy. Again, drill down to find the core of what made, or would make, you happy. Things like Fun and Adventure are values too, so do not discount them if they show up, but you will probably find a lot more than that, too.

Ask yourself if the value is only a means to an end, or if it is an end in itself. The 'end' will show your true value. For example, some people say that having money makes them happy - but is it the money, or the sense of security or freedom that they really value? Is it the status? Can you go beyond that? What is it about status that is so important? Make sure you really drill down with your answers.

And lastly, for the final question, what most fulfils you? For me, I really feel fulfilled by helping others in my work. What I enjoy about that is Helping, Learning, Teaching and Overcoming Challenges. Look at what the values behind what most fulfils you might be. Again, drill down deeply to find the most accurate answers. Remember to use the list of values at the back of the book if you need to.

By now you should have a list of values that are important to you in some way or another. Do you see any patterns emerging? Values that show up time and time again? These will be your top core values. But these are general values, and although adhering to them will make you happier and more fulfilled as you go through your life, what most people do not tell you is that values can be contextual. For example, what you value in work may not be exactly the same as what you value in a relationship. But there will be a few driving values that show up in everything you do, and hopefully you will have identified a good list of them by now. So now it's time to do a value check.

Reflect and Refine

From your group of values which show up time and time again in the answers to the previous exercise, pick a top ten or fifteen. Now we're going to test them!

Sadly, a lot of people end up living their lives according to other people's values or other people's rulebooks. So for each of your values, ask yourself the following questions:

Is this your value? Or is it something you think *should be* your value? Is it one of the values of your parents or society, or is it actually yours? You will know, because when you look at that value, it should be something that stirs you with positive emotions.

It might help to say the word slowly to yourself, and really consider it, and then see how your body and your mind react. Do you feel comforted, excited or passionate about that value? Is it something you want to live by for the rest of your life? Discount any values that seem imposed upon you and aren't really yours.

Now that you have your true top values, we are going to see which are the most important to you out of them all. The idea behind this is not to reduce your life to a top five, or a top three, or a single value, as we are all complex individuals. But the idea of arranging them in some way is to make it easier to know what your core values are - so you can check that you are adhering to them in what you do with your life.

So, get a pair of scissors, cut up some some rectangles of paper and write each value on one separate piece that you have cut up. Arrange the pieces of paper in a vertical line, roughly in the order that you believe they should be, with the things you think you value most of all at the top. Now we are going to test the values against each other.

Start with the bottom value in your line and ask yourself how it compares to the value directly above it, by asking the question:

"What if I could have X, but not Y?
Would that be OK with me?"

For example, if you had 'Security' at the bottom of your list and 'Helping Others' just above it, ask yourself "What if I could have security, but not be able to help others? Would that be OK with me?" And then turn it around and ask "What if I could help others, but not have security? Would that be OK with me?"

Of course you will find that you want both things, but there will be an innate preference that will tell you which is more important.

The thought of giving one up in order to have the other will make you slightly more uneasy than if it were the other way around. If you find that one value feels more important than the other, then readjust its position in your line. Progress up the line comparing each value with the ones directly above and below it and repositioning them as you feel fit.

Remember, if you have changed the position of one of the values, make sure you compare it with its new neighbours. It is not unusual to find that one value leapfrogs its way from quite some way down the list to somewhere nearer the top. We are not always aware of what really matters to us most of all!

This exercise can take some time, but it is really worth doing if you want to be clear about what your top core values really are. Because when you are clear about that, then you can start adjusting your actual life to fit in with what is important for you. This is the only way that we can ever be truly fulfilled and happy - by living our values.

Take-aways:

- Establish your core values
- You're a winner, not a loser, for being a recovering addict
- Addiction and recovery are not shameful
- You have to take action to get the life you want
- Take as big, but manageable, steps as you can without risking your sobriety
- Living by your values is the key to being happy

"There can be no happiness if the things we believe in are different from the things we do."

- Freya Stark

Chapter Four

Turn the Glass Over

You will be familiar with the question: "Is the glass half empty or half full?" I always think it's quite funny to think of this in relation to alcoholics, because I am pretty sure that neither would be an acceptable answer for us! We want the glass full to the brim, and a second lined up on the bar already, thank you very much. Plus a bottle stowed away in our clothing and/or in our bag, if you were anything like me.

Of course the question is designed to investigate what sort of attitude you have, whether you are naturally pessimistic or optimistic. And I would like to talk about attitude, because this is another stumbling block for many alcoholics and drug addicts.

Especially in early recovery, but even after some time has passed, many alcoholics and drug addicts look at not drinking or drugging any longer from the wrong perspective. They feel like they are missing out by giving up that lifestyle and their substance of choice. And all that does is lead to bitterness, and possibly even relapse. Of course we are happy to escape all the chaos and negative consequences that our addiction brings, but we yearn to be able to drink like normal people, or to occasionally take drugs in a more recreational way, as we may see other people doing with impunity.

We can spend our sobriety embittered by the fact that we 'can't have a good time' any more, or worrying that we are boring. But actually these are myths that it would serve you well to jettison from your mind. No one who knows me would ever describe me as boring. I actually do accompany friends to the pub and I am always the one who is laughing the loudest at our table.

I see myself as free in my sobriety, rather than restricted. Yet I have been guilty of the 'glass half empty' attitude too. I remember when I was in my twenties, I ended up in detox centres a few times, and I was *always* the youngest person there. Sadly, my drinking destroyed my health to such an extent that I had to be hospitalised on and off throughout my twenties. The same was true of the alcohol services I attended - I tended to be the only young face among a lot of older people. Now at the time I thought to myself "How can I have screwed myself up so badly at such a young age? Why couldn't I have lasted longer?" I refused to get sober, even though I saw the damage it was causing, because I could not bear the thought of having to live the rest of my life never drinking again.

'Sober' was a dirty word for me; and I desperately tried controlling my intake for several years, because I was not going to be someone who was *sober*. The very word conjured up boring people with no social lives who preferred knitting to a good night out. There was no way I was resigning myself to that fate at such a young age. Of course, controlled drinking didn't work and I did end up going sober after all - and at quite a young age compared to most alcoholics who find recovery.

The way I see it now, I am absolutely delighted that I managed to get sober so young in comparison to the average addict. Because it means that I can spend more of my life free, liberated from my addiction - and actually doing enjoyable things, rather than scrabbling around in the dirt of my chaotic illness. I am grateful that my body and mind gave out so young, as it gave me the opportunity to clean up and change my life.

At whatever age we manage to finally get clean, we should be utterly grateful that we got sober at all, rather than dying from this awful illness, as many do.

So, yes, I was happy that I was sober; but making up my mind that I was happy to be sober *all of the time* was another story entirely. And instead of taking a 'glass half full' or 'glass half empty' attitude, I had to turn the glass over and think about things in an entirely new way. I had to do a complete 360 on the issue. It was really no good putting down the drink and then not being totally happy about it. I would have always been resentful of my new life. So instead, I considered all the facts around my addiction and looked at how I felt about drinking and people who drank, too.

Now the number one fact that comes first in all of this is that I *can not* drink. When I was trying to rationalise why I should be able to control my drinking, I thought to myself of the days before it became such a big problem. When I was in my teens, drinking was fun. Nothing but fun and laughs, really. When I look back, I realise that actually I had always had a slightly different attitude to alcohol from most of my peers. Alcohol was probably more important to me than it was to many of my friends; and even among my mates who started drinking as young as I did, I was usually the one drinking them under the table. There were some clues in there, now that I look back on it. So it wasn't all as rosy and consequence-free as my selective memory would have me believe. *But* for the most part, drinking was a good laugh and we had a lot of fun.

Even when my drinking first became problematic, there were no serious consequences that couldn't be easily mended. I did not yet have that overwhelming obsession with alcohol. It didn't rule my life in the same way it did when I came towards the end of my active addiction. The fact that I had not always seemed to have been an addict somehow gave me a false sense that maybe I could go back to those times again. If only I were to go back to drinking beer, or perhaps I could just drink at weekends.

In those confused days of trying to control my drinking, I did not understand that it was too late to return to not being addicted. Once you have become addicted, that is it. No amount of wishing or euphoric recall can return your physiology, your neurology or your mind to that of a 'normal' drinker. I am aware that

I have been talking a lot about drinking, but I think it is clear that this is equally true of drugs. Once you have crossed the line from recreational use into addiction, there is no returning. And so the only thing to be done is to accept that fact, and to move on and live with the situation as it is now.

So that was a large part of the battle won, accepting that this was the way it was going to be from now on. I was going to be a non-drinker. But I wasn't happy about that fact at first. I was happy to be a normal person in the daytime, getting on with my life without needing a drink just to stop the shakes. But when it came to socialising it was another story. I think, in a way, it is a little bit easier for you drug users to avoid temptation. Of course it is easy for you to get drugs if you know where to get them, or who to ask, but they are not usually pushed in your face to the same extent that alcohol is. People do not generally think of you as odd if you refuse to take drugs socially, and you are unlikely to be encouraged to 'lighten up' or 'just have one', as people trying to stay alcohol-free often are.

In the UK especially, we have a very strong drinking culture and sadly we have come to a situation where a hangover is a badge of honour among young people. In Britain, births, weddings and deaths are all accompanied by excessive drinking rituals - and even just a social meal out with a friend or partner is usually accompanied by alcohol. The pub is the social hub of our communities more so than anything else, and these days people think you are somewhat strange if you do not drink.

I often think it is odd how modern society thinks it is perfectly acceptable for people to get so plastered that they forget where they are and can not walk or talk properly. And yet if you plied yourself with heroin and got into a state in the middle of the street, people would certainly stop and stare. It seems crazy that one form of intoxication is seen as perfectly reasonable and another is not. In my eyes, society needs to change its attitude -

but then that is a manifesto for another day entirely. The point is, alcohol is everywhere around you and unless you want to emigrate to Dubai, it is time to deal with it.

This also means that you need to separate your own drinking habits from those of everyone else. I am not particularly happy about our binge culture, but that is not my problem. My problem is me, and my own relationship to alcohol, and that is what you should be focussing on too.

When I got sober for good, I happened to be with a partner who drank every day. I actually do not think my partner was an alcoholic, but he certainly had an unhealthy relationship with alcohol. At first I tried to talk to him about it for his 'own good'. I pointed out how unhealthy his everyday drinking habit was and told him I was worried about it. Did anyone ever do that to you? Did it make a blind bit of difference? No, it didn't to him either - and I was just wasting my energy worrying about him as well as me. I had to separate my feelings about *him* drinking from my own problems with alcohol, because I can only deal with my *own* problems.

Lots of people can hardly believe I managed to find recovery despite living with someone who was drinking every day, but it can be done if you have the right attitude. Whether you actually want to stay with someone who is drinking or using drugs is something you will have to consider for yourself. There may be things about the company, the lifestyle, their behaviour, or any other accompanying problems, that you would prefer not to have in your life when you are sober. But if you take the attitude that I have, you can get sober and be happy about it, no matter what anyone else around you is doing.

This is particularly helpful for those of you who are stuck in situations where there is a lot of drinking or drug-taking around you, whether it is at work, in your local area or within your family. Do not believe that it can not be done, because it can and I can honestly say that my ex-partner's drinking never once tempted me to drink, because I held the attitude that 'alcohol and *me*' was my problem, not alcohol and anyone else. If anyone else close to me had an unhealthy relationship with drink or drugs, that was their issue, perhaps, but certainly not mine. I could tell them how I felt about it, but that once my concerns had been aired, I would have to leave it alone and focus on my own recovery.

So what do you do about your attitude to drinking or drugs? How do you get to that space where you are really not tempted and can have it around you and be quite comfortable about it? Where you do not feel that you are missing out by not having a few drinks, doing a few lines, or having a little smoke?

A strange thing happened to me when I was newly sober. I went to a support group very regularly in my early days, because I knew I couldn't stay sober initially on my own. I knew I would not be able to trust myself so early on in sobriety, before I had had the chance to work on myself and my attitude.

I was coming out of a meeting in Camden Town on a Friday night. If anyone is unfamiliar with Camden, it is a part of London that is pretty busy most of the time, but is particularly bustling at weekends. On a Friday night, people are spilling out of the bars and pubs onto the pavement. Lots of people are having a drink and enjoying themselves fairly noisily. As I was leaving the meeting, I walked past a group of young men who had clearly been drinking. One of them was hugging another, who was barely standing upright, and slurring "I love you, maaan," in that drunken way that I'm sure we would all recognise.

I felt the emptiness, the unreality of those words, said only because of the alcohol running through the young man's veins.

I didn't know whether these men were total strangers, close friends, brothers, colleagues or simply acquaintances. Whether, without the alcohol, that man did love the other is, in a way, completely unimportant.

Those words were void of actual love because they were only said under the influence.

I had just come from a room where I had received warm hugs from complete strangers. I'd had understanding, acceptance and care shown to me by people whom I had never met before, giving me a cup of tea, a friendly welcome and a heartfelt kind word. Opening up to me, although we had only just met, and sharing their hopes, dreams and fears with me. And all done with all of us *entirely sober*.

This experience awakened me to what the reality was. Sober, everything was real. I know that a lot of us drank or took drugs to escape from reality, but in doing so we robbed ourselves of all the opportunities to enjoy all the good, real stuff.

I have *real* fun, these days, now I'm sober. Any fun I have is created by me, my relationships, my activities. It is not fake fun, like drinking and taking drugs is. My expressions are real and heartfelt. The good times really *are* good times. As I walked past the young men, I felt sad suddenly for people who would never really know what I felt. The people who would never tell a friend they loved them unless it was under the influence of drink. Alcohol was the medium that could bring about affection. None of it was real or raw.

Those of us who are clean and sober are living courageously; we are 'living real'! What an amazing thing. We can do all the other things that everyone else does, except we can do them for real. When we dance sober, we really lose ourselves. Not that fake dancing after a few drinks, where you look like an idiot and can't appreciate the music because it's all about being a bit squiffy. Sober dancing is *all* about the music, as it should be. It is all about the rhythm, the feelings, the reality. It's back to the roots of real experience.

And instead of being stuck down the pub talking nonsense with (or at) our mates, as sober people we can really listen to what people say, we can think about things with a clear head, we can (usually) respond with intelligence and use the brain we were given.

Whatever society seems to have turned into, do you see now that it's the sober people who have it good? When I am having a good time now, I am having it for real. When I laugh, it's because something is actually funny, not because I'm drunk. When I make love, all of the feelings, sensations and emotions are real. Every nerve tingles uninhibited, not dampened by alcohol. It is so much better than a drunken shag.

And my friendships are real too. Did you ever hang out with certain people - and, if you're honest about it, drinking was all you ever did together? Did you ever try hanging out with those people sober? Man, they are so boring, aren't they? Talking nonsense, repeating themselves, spouting the same old garbage, laughing at the same old jokes. Give me a sober person to hang out with any day of the week.

The truth is, it is not just pre-recovery alcoholics and drug addicts who are scared to live in full reality. Most social functions organised by non-addicts are 'lubricated' by a few drinks. Why? Because people are too scared to socialise sober!

A friend of mine was telling me about a teetotal wedding she once went to. Apparently the bride and groom had given up drinking for a period of time and wanted to have a sober wedding. According to my friend, these were not people with a drinking problem; they just wanted a break from drinking and wanted to have an alcohol-free wedding as part of that. As soon as the mother of the bride heard this, she was horrified and nearly vetoed the whole wedding!

Apparently, she tried everything to persuade the couple to serve drinks at the wedding. She used 'other people', 'expectations' and all sorts of other things as excuses as to why the happy couple should bend to her wishes. They didn't in the end, and the wedding went ahead with a dry bar and no alcohol - and my friend said that everyone had a wonderful day. I bet there were no fights or even cross words at *that* wedding!

It makes you think, doesn't it? Why on earth would someone be so desperate to change the wishes of the couple getting married and to insist on changing the arrangements for their day? Do you think she would have been as vocal about the colour of the tablecloths or the flowers in the bouquet? Probably not. People are scared of sobriety, I think; and that is why non-drinkers are looked upon as a bit weird. Happily I have seen the other side of things - and the cool people are those who dare to live sober, who dare to dance, laugh, sing, make love, and do everything else in full reality.

I no longer care what people think about me not drinking, because I am the one from whose eyes the veil has been lifted. Alcohol is a poison, a toxin, and anyone who has ever had a hangover can attest to that being true. Being intoxicated is not a natural state at all, and whatever society chooses to believe because it is afraid, we know very different. You do not have to have alcohol to have fun. Ever seen a six-year-old drinking? No - and yet they have more fun than the lot of us. As we grow up, we learn to become self-conscious - and drinking is a quick fix for that. The good news is that we can learn to overcome that self-consciousness and to do things despite it; and those of us who are sober are the only ones who have the courage to actually do that. We are the brave ones - the people who choose to live clean and sober. How lucky we are to have this chance that few others ever get.

Now I mentioned a few activities in the previous paragraphs that *you* may have felt a little wary of doing sober, if you have not done them sober for a long time.

Because I was an alcoholic from a very young age, there were a lot of things on that list that I had never, *ever* done sober. And I will admit that the thought of doing them did fill me with some trepidation at first. But the thing is, *none* of those things were as scary as I first thought they would be. In fact when you've done them a few times, they cease to hold any fear at all. And anything that you do *despite* being a little scared at the time, simply builds your character.

I will just add a little disclaimer here. I am perfectly comfortable spending time down the pub these days, although I do not go nearly as much as I used to! I know quite a few people who are sober and who do not really feel comfortable socialising down the pub or in environments where there is a lot of alcohol, or if there are drugs about.

I do not know if their reluctance is because these environments are far too associated in their minds with triggers for using for them to ever be comfortable. All I will say is, if it really makes you feel uncomfortable and uneasy, then do not do it. Sobriety is about fun and enjoying yourself, not about torturing yourself or trying to prove a point. It may be possible at some point, but if you're not enjoying it, and it gives you nothing, there is no point in forcing the issue. You don't have to do anything you don't want to - being clean and sober is about being liberated, not about being restricted and trapped.

I have never felt tempted to drink in situations where there is a lot of drink flowing, but sometimes I find them unpleasant.

For example, I went to the Notting Hill Carnival when I was newly sober. For anyone who doesn't know it, it is a massive party and people are usually drinking from early in the morning. The people I went with had been drinking steadily all day and I spent about five hours there, but by the time it reached about 5pm, I decided I had to leave.

It wasn't that I was tempted, but rather that the people around me were becoming obnoxious and irritating, and I knew that I wouldn't have fun if I stayed there and listened to them talking rubbish and acting all silly. So, in situations such as that, which luckily don't happen very often, I do sometimes bail out early. I had had a nice five hours of sober partying but I knew staying any longer would be a bad idea.

So it wasn't that it was me being sober and boring - it was that they were drunk and boring! And life is far too short to waste my time being bored.

So apart from the occasional early exit, which is usually due to the boring company of others, I enjoy all the social stuff that I would as a social drinker - except I do it full-throttle, for real, without a cosy beer overcoat to hide behind. In fact as long as people around me are not absolutely plastered, I am often the one who is last to go home on a night out.

Now if any of you think being sober is boring after reading this chapter, I would be quite surprised; but of course I have included a few exercises to help you to make these attitudes your own. So get on with the following exercises and you can be even happier and even more sociable sober than you ever were drunk or on drugs.

Exercises

The Accepting Addict

Human beings are so used to moaning about things, that it is almost second nature to us. We moan about the weather, the length of queues, how our hair is never quite right and how expensive things are these days. We moan about everything and anything.

The ridiculous thing is that we often complain most of all about things that we have absolutely no power to change. Does whining about the rain mean that the sun will suddenly come out? Will our whinging suddenly reduce the supermarket queue snaking away in front of us? No, it won't. And that's why it's not only a waste of time, but a drain on our energy.

We are indulging in pointless negativity and wishing our lives away when we focus on things that we are unable to change. We would be far better off accepting those things for what they are, and instead, focusing our energies on what it *is* within our power to change.

So let's start with our thoughts about drinking and drugging. Is it any good bemoaning the fact that you are one of those people who can not take alcohol or drugs at all? Will that change the past or change the future? Will it make you any happier to worry about something you can't change? No? If you ever think your situation is worth complaining about anyway, then tell yourself the following things:

"Fighting the facts is a waste of time and energy."

"The more time I spend on unproductive things, the less time I have to do brilliant things."

"Reacting to things I can not change does not serve me."

You can use the same acceptance tactic if you have other people around you who are still drinking or taking drugs, and you feel it is making your life more difficult. Key phrases to focus on include:

"I can not change anyone except myself."

"Other people's problems are none of my business, unless they ask for help"

"I need all of my energy to deal with my own sobriety."

"Nothing anyone does, or says, can make me pick up a drink or drug."

That final one is particularly important if you are in a situation where there are drugs or alcohol around you. It is utterly true as well. Unless someone ties you down and forces substances into you physically, they can not make you pick up. If you choose to, then that's your choice. But no-one can make you do anything you don't choose to do.

Next, it is time to refocus your energies on learning how to be happy now that you are clean, sober and liberated from addictive behaviours. Realise at a deep level that all I said in the previous chapter is true - you can look forward to some amazing and totally real experiences that are a hundred times better than living in a fake reality, if you do what it takes and stick with sobriety.

If you ever get stuck on thoughts trying to pull you back into negativity, ask yourself "Where do I want to be?" Think about the end you have in mind - that is to be in recovery and to be happy, right? Think about how your reactions will contribute to that. Will moaning and complaining get you there or will working on turning your attitude get you there? Go with what is effective. It's the only way.

And if you find yourself drifting off into the feeling that this is all unfair or negative, just be aware of those thoughts rather than getting caught up in them. It may help to say to yourself:

"I notice I am having the thought that this unfair."

"I am aware that I feel like moaning."

"This is only a thought. I do not have to act on it."

Don't start telling yourself off if unwanted thoughts and reactions popping into your mind. It is perfectly normal for this to happen at first. Just practice being non-judging of those thoughts, observing them as thoughts and not as things that you have to get caught up in. Thoughts, after all, are only thoughts - nothing says you have to do what they say.

Be a Sober Daredevil!

I have already acknowledged that we are pretty brave souls deciding to be sober and to experience things in their full and glorious reality while others are hampered by self-consciousness and unease.

The joy of it is that experiencing these things is totally worth working through the trepidation for.

This exercise is designed to show you why your fears exist, and then to take steps to act, despite not feeling certain of your footing. So just take a deep breath and we'll begin.

First, pick something you feel quite nervous of doing sober. We will then go through the elements of it that cause the fear and make a plan to do it anyway.

Firstly, fear of taking action is usually caused by one of four things. We will use the rather apposite acronym C.R.U.D to help you remember what they are:

Chattering mind — The stories your mind tells you about why you can't do things. False beliefs about yourself. Random negative thoughts or self-talk.

Really big goals — When you feel overwhelmed because the goal feels too big, or too much.

Unwillingness to face discomfort — The unwillingness to sacrifice a bit of comfort or certainty for the greater good of achieving your goal.

| **D**on't haves | Lacking the resources, support or tools you need. |

I'd like you to list the things that are holding you back and making you feel nervous when you think of trying something sober. I will run through the exercise using dancing sober as an example.

C: I tell myself I will look silly. Other people are better dancers than me. What if I have two left feet? I'm probably too old to start dancing now anyway. People might laugh at me.

R: I have never been dancing sober before. I don't think I could do it somewhere where other people are drinking.

U: I will feel too self-conscious.

D: I don't have anyone to dance with; I don't know which clubs have good music.

So, the next step is to look at how we will combat these objections and get you to achieve your sober goal anyway. We will run them through the C.O.M.B.A.T Matrix, in order to make them manageable.

Clarify what your mind is trying to give you.

Is it a form of protection? Acknowledge that your mind is just trying to help and thank it for that.

Objectively accept the feelings.

You could even measure them on a scale if it helps. How uncomfortable do you feel out of 10?

Mentally Re-frame.

> Look for evidence against your fears, look for comparisons, reasons to doubt your previous judgements and new meanings you can form.

Break the goal down into manageable chunks.

> Make mini-goals or plan out steps to make the task seem smaller and easier.

Additional support.

> Gather resources and prepare; ask for help if necessary.

Totally realise the importance of the goal and how it is linked to your values and living them.

> And I mean Totally with a capital 'T'. This is the absolute seal of why you are going to do this thing anyway, despite your fears.

Here is the example of dancing sober, run through the C.O.M.B.A.T Matrix:

C: I know my mind is trying to keep me from feeling discomfort. It wants to keep me safe. It wants to keep me from embarrassing myself. I thank it for trying to protect me.

O: I am feeling anxiety. I think my anxiety is about 7 out of 10 on this issue.

M: I'm not as scared as when I had to take my driving test, and I still managed that. Who says I'm too old? What does that mean anyway? Does it even matter if I can't dance - I'm not in a competition, it's just a bit of fun. There are probably many positive experiences I have been afraid of, before I had them. It's not something I'm afraid of, it's just unfamiliar. There is really nothing to be scared of - I'm not going to be eaten by a tiger on the dance floor. Probably no-one will even notice I'm sober anyway! I am not the centre of the world - no-one will care if I'm dancing or not.

B: I will have a bit of a boogie in the comfort of my room before I go. I will plan to go for an hour and have an exit strategy if I need one. I could go to a sober club night.

A: I am going to call my friend and ask her advice on the club with the best music, or one that is quieter. I will invite her and some other friends to go with me.

T: Being able to dance will be incredibly enjoyable. It will show I am courageous and independent, which are two of my top values. Maybe I will make new friends or develop a skill. I will be proud of myself and feel more like I can live a normal life. It will show I can still enjoy myself sober. It will be another massive achievement on my recovery journey! Damn it, I'm doing this!

In the end, we all have to do things that we are not entirely comfortable with at times. But when they really matter to us, because they will fit in with our values and improve our self-confidence or enhance our lives, it is always worth doing them.

You'll be glad to know that I dance sober these days, thanks to using this technique. I was always into music and going to gigs. I would have missed some amazing performances if I hadn't gone for it sober. I guess I'm a better dancer when I don't fall down half-way through.

If you are still feeling stuck, a really big final 'push' question you can ask yourself is:

> "Do I really want to be forever limited by difficult thoughts and feelings? Would I not prefer to move forward and break the pattern so that I can feel proud, happy and more able to take on challenges one after the other?"

Who wouldn't answer "Yes!" to that?

Take-aways:

- The best recovery comes from accepting your sobriety
- Sober people have real, exhilarating, amazing fun
- Sobriety is a new freedom in life rather than a restriction
- No-one and nothing can jeopardise your sobriety without your permission
- Focus your energies on meeting sober challenges
- Prepare yourself to do a few uncomfortable things and your sober life will expand exponentially
- Challenge your old attitudes and ways of thinking

> "Accept challenges, so that you may feel the exhilaration of victory."
>
> - George S. Patton

Chapter Five

Snow White and the Seven Dwarves

There is absolutely no point making peace with the past, and losing that feeling of shame and guilt, if you're not going to construct a new life that you are proud of.

It is completely counter-intuitive to heal from your past and then go on living your life in a negative way. I know some people who are sober, but they keep on doing the wrong things; and while I'm proud of them for being sober - after all it is a massively difficult thing to do to escape addiction - I can't help but think that they're storing up problems for themselves in the end.

One of the most wonderful things about my own recovery is that I go to bed every day with an amazing peace of mind and that comes from having done the right thing.

I once heard comedian Jack Dee describe his idea of Hell. He said he imagined it was like a cinema, where your life was replayed on a big screen, second-by-second in front of everyone you have ever known. Nothing missed out, nothing edited; everything there in full, glorious Technicolor for everyone to see.

I remember when I was in active addiction, just hearing him joke about that made me cringe at the thought of it. There were so many lies I'd told, so many things I had done that I wouldn't want anyone else to see or know about; so many secrets, so many bad ways of behaving and so many awful things I had said and done. I wouldn't have wanted my next-door neighbour or my postman to see it, let alone my mother or father, or my friends.

And I thought about that image of Hell again when I was a year into being sober. And during that year, I can genuinely say, there was nothing in there that I would be ashamed of anyone seeing or knowing about. Of course, I wouldn't have wanted everyone to see all of it, just on grounds of privacy, but there was truly nothing in there that I felt bad about, or that showed me behaving maliciously or in bad spirit.

But of course that's not to say that I didn't make any mistakes. Sure, I screwed up. I had moments where I lost it, or was unfair, angry, moody or not really my ideal self. I had arguments in that time, and made poor judgements or got sucked into negative emotions. But there was nothing that I could be hard on myself for, nothing that anyone could pick on and say I had behaved shabbily. Anything I did fall down on, I tried to make up for, and I apologised when I saw it was right to do so. I was as 'snow white' as I possibly could be.

It was a massive moment for me when I realised that I have a totally clear conscience today. If things don't work out, it's not because I haven't tried my best and it's not because I have been dishonest, selfish, cruel or uncaring.

So now, I would be proud to have my film play up there on that giant screen for all the world to see. Of course, that would mean that the first, troubled part of my life would also be up there to be judged, but I would hope that, by now, my 'movie' would be a story of redemption. Anything I did in the bad old days would be seen in the light of the film ending with me becoming a better person and turning my life around. And that is a great and wonderful thing, rather than the hellish fate it would have been for me before.

And part of the reason that I am proud of my life story these days is that I have committed to always doing the right things. Going forward, my mission in life has been to do my absolute best and cultivate all my good qualities at the same time as correcting my more negative behaviours.

And that's not been easy work sometimes. I have Borderline Personality Disorder to contend with, which means that I can be hyper-emotional if I don't keep myself in check. If I do the wrong thing, I can rapidly start going in a downward spiral of negativity, where each bad thought or reaction leads onto another. But my utter willingness to become the person I was always meant to be has meant that I have been happy to do the work necessary to keep on improving myself.

And the gift that I get from that? When I go to bed at night, I can feel truly proud and positive about everything I have done that day. Knowing I have done the right thing can counter any moments of upset I might have. No matter how bad the day has been, if I know I have done the right thing, I don't stay awake dwelling on the negatives for too long.

Doing the right thing also has an additional benefit. The more right things I do, the more good things happen to me. Life is life - bad and unexpected things will always happen out of the blue, but for once I can say that they are none of my doing. And that can be a very comforting thought indeed, especially when you are experiencing a lot of pain.

Of course when you're coming from a long way back, it's a matter of progress - but taking the right steps forward, little by little, is going to get you going on the right path. No-one is, or will ever be, perfect. We all mess up. After all we're not robots.

But the importance lies in trying your best and if you do screw up, admit it and atone for it as soon as you can. I used to be afraid of the word 'sorry'. I would either use it all the time and not mean it - like when someone bumped into me or if I was trying to disagree with someone in a tactful way. Or I would stubbornly refuse to admit that I was wrong, calling the sky green and the grass red before I would use that word. And while I don't like saying 'sorry' these days (because it means I have done something wrong to someone else), I will say it if I need to. I don't dread having to apologise these days either - I just take it as part of the process of doing the right thing. In fact, when I come to a realisation that I have been wrong, and I am truly sorry, I can't wait to see the person to apologise and make it up to them.

And most people will forgive you - after all how can you not forgive someone when you know that they're genuine and that they're trying their best to do the right thing?

So what are my top tips for improving your character? Well, it's just a matter of looking at the things you don't do so well and trying to change them. Poring over your weaknesses could potentially be quite a painful task, but if you approach it from a spirit of logic, acceptance and forgiveness, it can be easy and liberating rather than upsetting.

In fact it is much easier to change certain things about yourself when you look at them objectively, without getting caught up in emotional judgement. If you attach emotional values to your weaknesses, you may find you become defensive or upset about your less positive qualities, and that is completely unhelpful.

Stepping back and looking at yourself objectively is not only much more pleasant, but it puts you in control of changing things. If you can accept yourself first, it is easier to modify your behaviours, because you will have no reason to become defensive or hopeless. Think of it like a clinical evaluation of yourself rather than an exercise in beating yourself up.

Some of you might find that you are in denial about some of your less pleasant attributes. I will never forget the day when I realised I did in fact have a huge problem with anger. I'd always thought of myself as some *Little House on the Prairie* type, best suited to sewing and eating muffins. That was probably because I was horribly unassertive in my daily undertakings. But if someone hurt me, I lost it utterly. Several smashed-up phones and a multitude of dents in the wall are a testament to that. But I did realise it in the end; I even had a bit of a giggle at myself for denying the obvious evidence, and then I decided to work on it.

The exercises below will help you to work on your weaknesses and build up your positive traits.

Exercises

The Seven Dwarves

In the following exercise, I will give you a list of traits that a person might possess. And I want you to look at them honestly and non-judgementally and see if they might apply to you. What I mean by non-judgementally is that this is not an exercise for you to beat yourself up with. Please be totally objective, as you might be when labelling the colours of your clothes, or whether you like certain genres of music or not. Are you like this - or aren't you? It's as simple as that.

Go through the traits, one by one, and see if you can find any evidence for them in your life. When you have identified all the characteristics that you think apply to you, then look at how you might work on them. I want you to make a list of very practical ways that you can think of to start behaving more positively.

For example, with my anger issues, I made a list of steps I could take in order to sort the problem out. I did a lot of walking in the early days - it was pretty *angry* walking, as anyone who might have seen me stomping down the street would attest to, but it was a great starting place for not doing other negative things, such as throwing things or shouting my head off at someone. And it saved me a fortune in replacement phones. Another favourite trick of mine was putting on *Sabotage* by *The Beastie Boys* and bouncing on the bed for all I was worth, to let some of the anger out.

But I didn't just do physical things - those were often effective, but an even better way of reducing my angry reactions was to change my thinking on the issues. I tried to rationalise logically what I was angry about and see if I could solve it, rather than reacting with anger.

So, for example, if I felt angry about the way I'd been treated, it was often better to say my piece calmly to the other party. It was often a matter of proportion, too - usually I wouldn't get mad at one incident, but it was a series of things that I had let build up. And so I took steps to prevent that train of events happening again, by intervening earlier.

If it's too much to tackle all your least favourite parts of yourself at once, just pick out what I call your 'Seven Dwarves'. From the list of traits which apply to you, work out which seven of them are the least appealing parts of your personality, the areas where you are weakest, or the traits that you need to change the most urgently. For me personally, on a bad day I was Angry, Needy, Stubborn, Wilful, Moody, Over-sensitive and Impulsive.

So I've shared with you my worst bits. Now it's your turn. Go through the list of traits, one by one, and ask yourself:

Am I sometimes..(insert trait)..?

And if you are sometimes guilty of exhibiting that trait, ask yourself:

What could I do instead of being like that?

This is very, very important. There is no point listing all the weaknesses you have if you haven't made a plan to work on them too. Make a serious, structured plan for each. And really commit to changing those weaknesses into your strengths. You may think of others that I haven't listed - and that's great. Just add them to your list. And don't forget to congratulate yourself on the traits that you've avoided - we'll move onto looking at all your positive qualities later.

Are you sometimes...? What could you do instead?

Inconsiderate	Fussy	Whiny	Vengeful
Hypercritical	Greedy	Wilful	Cowardly
Argumentative	Grumpy	Worrisome	Cruel
Arrogant	Harsh	Possessive	Cynical
Begrudging	Angry	Needy	Dishonest
Bitchy	Impatient	Obsessive	Boastful
Domineering	Impulsive	Mean	Malicious
Bossy	Lazy	Patronizing	Intolerant
Untrustworthy	Pompous	Pessimistic	Miserly
Conceited	Indecisive	Cold	Irresponsible
Aggressive	Interfering	Moody	Jealous
Inconsistent	Over-emotional	Narrow-minded	Judgemental

The Seven Giants

Even your worst traits have some positive elements to them. There are very good reasons why we have 'negative' traits, otherwise there wouldn't be any point in having them! So, as an antidote to looking at your weaknesses, let's look at your Seven Dwarves and see in which contexts they might be looked at as Seven Giants instead.

In what ways could your 'weaknesses' be seen as useful or positive traits? How do they help you survive, and which parts of them do you want to keep? For example, my Stubbornness means that I am a great advocate for others, and my Impulsiveness means that my friends get lots of presents. So, how can you look at your weaknesses as strengths and useful mechanisms?

At the end of both exercises consolidate your plan for getting rid of the worst of your weaknesses, ensuring that you still have ways of getting your needs met. How could you achieve the same results that your Seven Dwarves used to give you, but in a more positive way?

Work out the steps you will take now. And I shouldn't need to remind you that making a list and writing it all out in pretty colours will not mean a thing if you don't take committed action to change.

Take-aways:

- Even your worst days can be good days when you do the right thing and have a clear conscience
- We all have negative traits for a reason, and in some circumstances they can be positive
- Don't criticise yourself - be objective about your flaws
- You need a plan of action if you seriously wish to strengthen your weaknesses

"Clear conscience never fears midnight knocking."

- Chinese Proverb

Chapter Six

I am not a Chocolate Biscuit

Did you ever hear anyone say "You are what you eat?" Lots of people probably think this is a wise and brilliant piece of advice - but not me. I think it's a load of nonsense. It's far too simplistic to be of any real value. Does eating a cheese sandwich or a chocolate biscuit or a bowl of spaghetti make you any of those things? Of course not. The actions of eating those things are just choices that you made at a certain point in time. Eating a biscuit is a choice, not a life sentence, leaving you forever condemned to *be* a chocolate biscuit! And I'd like you to think about your addiction, and your behaviours while living the addicted life, in the same way.

Now I don't know about you, but during my addiction I indulged in the sneakiest, most low-down behaviours imaginable. I acted worse than an animal in some cases. I was completely unreliable, untrustworthy and manipulative. Does that make me a sneaky old manipulative liar now? No. Does it make those behaviours *who I essentially am*? No. It makes me a person who made some unwise choices and did some regrettable things.

In some cases, the choices I made and the actions I took were diametrically opposed to who I actually am, and what matters to me, now that I'm sober - and the 'real' me is allowed to surface. I despise sneakiness and celebrate openness. I value truth and believe in honesty. So why did I do all that? Because I was making choices that allowed me to survive, the only way I knew how. I was ill and trying to protect myself.

Now that I am in recovery, I can actually live my values. In fact, when I meet people now who never knew me when I was an active alcoholic, they find it really hard to believe that I was ever that bad. You would never know I was a mad raving alkie by my behaviours now. And yet I haven't had a lobotomy or been struck by lightning or made a deal with God and been given a different soul. I am just behaving differently.

You see, you are NOT your behaviours. You are a unique human being who can choose from a number of options at any one time; a person who can choose which way to behave in any given circumstances.

Having made a choice doesn't commit you to living that way forever, and having acted a certain way doesn't preclude you from doing something completely differently next time.

And let me get another thing straight. Being an alcoholic, or any other type of addict, does not make you a bad person. All human beings are simply trying to find their way in life and tend to make the best choice available to them at the time, with the resources they have. It may be an awful choice in the end, it may be the most dreadful mistake ever, but it is the best you could do back then.

No-one sets out to deliberately screw up their life. We just do that sometimes because that's all we know how to do to handle things and to survive. We don't always have better resources or the ability to look at problems with a long-term perspective.

In my own case, I had no idea that I was actually suffering from a serious, yet treatable, anxiety disorder; so I had no idea how to get help for it. I chose drinking as it enabled me to function, to face the world and to carry on in life without being housebound. That was the best choice I could make at the time - the one that enabled me to survive and carry on.

Had I known all I know now about my disorder and alcoholism and addiction, would I make the same choice? Probably not. But now I have the knowledge and tools to help me make better choices. I didn't have that back then, so I am not going to criticise myself for choosing the behaviours that I did. I just didn't have any better resources at the time. And neither did you.

People drink and drug for all sorts of reasons - to hide from anxiety, depression or unbearable pain, to feel like they fit in, to cope with a difficult life, to relax, to let go. Or maybe it was all they knew, or they were brought up being taught and shown that it was a good thing to do, or an acceptable way to cope.

I have never heard of anyone developing and nurturing a drinking or drug problem solely to piss everyone off or to slowly kill themselves. It was always a decision (largely unconscious) made out of the intention of coping, and therefore it had a positive intention, however unwise or misguided.

Change

So what about when you realise that things can't go on the way they have been, and you need to make different choices and to behave in different ways? The first step is to seek out other options to your old ways of behaving, and to look at different choices that might get you to your outcome. It is vital to have a wide range of other options available, or to discover them if you don't know what they might be yet.

Going back to the chocolate biscuit analogy; what if you realised that eating choccie biccies was doing you no good and you wanted to stop eating them, but they were all you had in the cupboard? What if you didn't know there was anything else to eat other than chocolate biscuits? Or your local shop was stocked to the brim with chocolate biscuits and nothing else? It wouldn't be very easy to change, would it?

So it comes down to searching far and wide for other options - and some of these may be things you had never considered before, or options you never believed would be right for you. The only thing to do is to try other things, to expand your mind to possibilities and give yourself the greatest number of options you could possibly have.

It is easier to take advantage of the right options when you have a whole range of possibilities in front of you, rather than just one or two things you could do. If you find the number of options overwhelming, then you can whittle them down later to a size that feels comfortable for you. But it is better to have all the options available first; otherwise you never know what you might be missing out on.

For example, when I eventually did find out that I had Social Anxiety Disorder, I now knew that I had to sort that out if I was going to make a serious job of getting sober. But I limited myself to a few things that felt safe for me. And guess what - they didn't work! I tried counselling, anti-anxiety medication, Cognitive Behaviour Therapy (CBT) and all the things that were mainstream at the time. But not one of them fit the bill. They may have had some limited positive impact, but never enough to solve my problem and so I was still stuck in my old behaviour of being petrified - and drinking to cope.

It was only after I started thinking outside of the box that I was eventually cured of my disorder. Someone close to me asked me if I had ever considered hypnotherapy or Neuro-linguistic Programming (NLP). Of course I hadn't - that was quackish nonsense surely. But out of desperation, I booked an appointment with an NLP Hypnotherapist, and the rest is history.

Within ninety minutes my disorder was gone, using a mixture of NLP and the Emotional Freedom Technique (EFT), which is a tapping protocol. Let me say, even sitting there in the chair in that practitioner's office, I was already prepared for disappointment when he asked me to start tapping with my fingers on my different parts of my body. I was beyond amazed to find that it actually worked. Thankfully, I had found a cure for my anxiety disorder and I'm now lucky enough to able to use this tool to help numerous other people to overcome their anxiety disorders too.

I never would have managed to get better if I hadn't considered all of the options, even those that I thought would never work. But did that mean I stopped drinking from that point onwards? Now that I had acknowledged the damage that my drinking was doing, and had got rid of my original reason for drinking, surely it would be easy? But no. I was destined to be a relapser for a long time after that.

Some people may argue that once you've realised you're an alcoholic or have finally come to realise that your drug addiction has to come to an end, then doesn't that make it your own fault when you relapse? If you have the knowledge that your addiction is causing all sorts of problems, and you need to change, doesn't that mean that you are a bad person for not sorting yourself out? Well no, because in order to modify any behaviour, you need to have three things: knowledge, options and tools. You will be missing some vital component in recovery of you're lacking any of those.

Back when I was Relapse Queen, I certainly knew all the cruddy stuff about relapse - I knew that I had to sort my drinking out, and I was determined to do it. I also had options. But I lacked tools. And this meant that no matter how much I knew and how many options were given to me, I still could not change my behaviours to what I really wanted. So I had to get my hands on some tools for living sober, for moving on and for living my daily life in a better way.

Now that I have all three things, my life is wonderful. I have the possibility of choosing all the behaviours that truly align with my core values. I can really be me! And that's all because I got hold of the three things that would allow me to have the freedom to choose what I do and who I want to be.

I am not stuck being a chocolate biscuit, nor an active alcoholic, nor any of those things that are not really who I am; they were only an expression of not knowing what else to do, and not having the means to do anything else.

We can create our own path

The super-fantastic news is that once you make a start on living your new behaviours, all of your future choices become influenced by the positive consequences of the ones you made before, making it even easier for you to maintain the momentum.

You know how you sometimes kept drinking or using because the guilt of the night before? Well, you can replace that negative spiral with a positive one, when you keep doing the right thing and getting good results. If you can commit to your new behaviours, it just becomes easier and easier, and more and more roads will open up in front of you to help you to carry on with your good choices.

You're probably tired of the chocolate biscuit analogy, so I'll move onto atlases to show you what I mean. Not as tasty, but probably more useful.

If you knew that you had to get from London to New York by tonight, what is the first thing you might do? If you were making a sensible choice, you'd probably start heading to Heathrow Airport to catch a flight. Now, you are left with a few choices there as well - which form of transport would you like to use?

If you chose to walk, you would be losing valuable time, and you might be limited by the number of flights available to you when you got there. Whereas if you travelled by car or train, you'd probably get there early enough to have more options available.

Likewise, on the journey to the airport, you could choose to get your atlas out, and if you made the right choices, each road or turning you took would take you closer and closer to Heathrow. And the nearer you got to the airport, at each junction you came to, the roads there would be more likely to lead to the airport than before. Whereas if you forgot to take an atlas, started heading the wrong way and took the motorway up to Scotland, all the other junctions you came to would be likely to lead you further and further northwards and further away from where you needed to be.

Now this doesn't mean that you can't find your way back from one or two wrong turnings, but isn't it even easier for you to find better choices once you start off well?

Some of you might have said "Well I wouldn't be heading to Heathrow anyway. I'd have jumped in a private jet!" I like you, because you are an out-of-the box thinker and that will serve you well in other ways. You can create options from out of nowhere when you think like that, and more surprising opportunities should open themselves up to you as a result.

Either way, the series of choices you make is important, as they open you up to more good options at the next stage.

Sometimes we have to force ourselves to make the right choices, but the rewards are always there when we do.

One of my friends really hates going to bed early, but he needs seven hours of sleep to be at his best. If he has any less than seven hours sleep, he struggles to get up in the morning. While he would rather stay up and be a night owl, if he has an important business meeting or an appointment early the next day, he will make the effort to go to bed early.

Now if he chooses to go to bed late, because that's what he feels like doing, he might struggle to get up, miss his meeting and maybe not get a business deal as a result. Whereas if he decides to go to bed early, he can be sure of getting up on time, having time to prepare himself and look his best for the meeting. He might then impress the client, and who knows where that could lead? A dedicated repeat customer, a new network through that customer, recommendations, more money. All sorts of things might happen as a result of making the right choice early on and following it through.

Although it meant using a certain amount of self-discipline, once my friend had practised going to bed early a few times and had seen how much better it was for him and his life overall, he saw that it was worth the sacrifice of a bit of late night telly.

And by doing it a handful of times, it became easier to do the next time, as he learnt all the things that would help him along the way; and it became a habit, rather than an effort.

Those of you who choose to do the right thing, even when it is difficult to do so at first, will find that your lives are richer and full of more opportunities than before. And the more you act in this way, the easier it will become to be consistent with your new choices.

Exercises

The Change Challenge

Most people are not particularly used to thinking outside of the box. One of the reasons why people find it so hard to change is that they truly believe they have no choice! It's easy to believe that, especially if you have been stuck on the hamster wheel of addiction and have been feeling trapped on it for a long time.

Sometimes when I ask my clients to come up with a list of options for something they want to change, they find it incredibly difficult to think of more than a few. It's not that they don't want to change, but sometimes they genuinely can not see the wood for the trees.

During active addiction, our brains become so focused on our substance of choice that it is often difficult to think of much else. As a lot of you will know, addiction not only takes over your life, but your mind, too.

Here is a challenge for you; a way of stretching your brain and helping it to work on finding all the options it can possibly find in various different scenarios.

First, ask a friend about something they want to change or a dilemma that they have. You could even imagine a person if you don't want to ask anyone, and invent a problem for them.

Now I want you to make a list of 25 options they could potentially choose from to solve their problem. These options can range from sensible to downright silly, as long as you have 25. The point of the exercise is to become creative. Some people find they can come up with some genius ideas using this method.

I'll give you a completely fictional example. My fictional friend, Fred, wants to go on holiday to France but he hasn't got any money. Typical fictional friend.

Here are 25 ways he could solve his problem:

1. Get a part-time job to save up money
2. Pretend to be a hotel inspector to get a free room
3. Swim across the channel and camp on the beach
4. Stow away in the boot of a car
5. Qualify for the Tour de France
6. Sell his swanky TV to get the money
7. Borrow the money from his best friend
8. Start dating a French lady and go with her when she visits her family
9. Become the French Ambassador
10. Write a French cookery book and get paid by the publishers to promote it overseas
11. Join a band who want to tap into the French market
12. Write to Richard Branson and ask for a free flight
13. Pretend to be an illegal immigrant and get transported 'back' to France
14. Join a house-swap programme and swap with someone in France

15. Get scouted by Olympic Marseilles FC
16. Get employed as an au pair in France
17. Ask all his friends to see if anyone knows people he can stay with gratis
18. Enter loads of competitions until he eventually wins a holiday
19. Become a long-distance lorry driver that exports to France
20. Save a pound a day until he has enough money
21. Become a foreign exchange student
22. Don't go on holiday at all - recreate France in his sitting room with appropriate cuisine and decorate the sofa with tricolores
23. Mail himself to France by courier
24. Join the army and ask to be stationed in France
25. Get employed as a cheese-taster and insist on going to Brie for research purposes

As I said, the point of this is not to look for totally realistic options at first, but just to get your creative mind working. Sometimes after thinking of lots of silly options, you will come up with a genius idea. Don't ask me why - it is just the way the brain works. The more you challenge your brain, the more you enable it to be creative. So, do the above exercise to get your creative muscle working.

And then, when you've practised by using a fictional example, think of something real that you would like to change, or a problem you would like to solve. Make yourself think of at least 25 options for what you could do, in the same way.

Sow the Seeds

The following exercise is useful for when you have identified something that you want to change. Maybe it is a behaviour or a way of thinking or being.

Please don't roll your eyes at me when I mention 'affirmations'. Research in the scientific community has shown that affirmations actually make us healthier, happier individuals and can help us to change our behaviours in the long-term.

Make a list of affirmations you can use for changing your behaviour. It is important that these affirmations are:

- Stated in the present tense
- Relate to the behaviours you want to take on, not those you want to jettison.

Don't state them as 'wishes' or 'I will' statements. State them as if they are already true. And don't state the thing you want to avoid doing, state the thing that you want to become. For example, if you wanted to change your fiery temper don't state "I wish I could/I will stop losing my temper." Instead, you could choose the affirmation: "I am in control of my temper at all times" or maybe "I am good-tempered and patient."

Or if you wanted to become less critical of others, you could use the affirmation: "I am a tolerant person" or "I respect and accept everyone I meet." You could use the qualities you chose to work on in the previous chapter - that would be a great place to start.

There are a couple of ways of using these affirmations. Research has shown that affirmations tend to be particularly effective at raising your mood if used when you first wake in the morning. You could even say them in the mirror to yourself, although if you find that you get distracted or feel self-conscious doing that, it is fine just to say them to yourself in your head.

Some people find it helpful to physically write out their affirmations. You can either write them out once a day in a journal or write them on a piece of paper, keeping it in a place where you will look several times a day, such as your purse or wallet. You can then read the affirmations throughout the day, whenever you look in that particular place.

Another option is to say your affirmations just before you go to bed - studies have shown that learning occurs best when we have a break from doing anything, so sleeping gives your brain the perfect opportunity to process your affirmations while you rest.

Now before you get all cynical, I am not one of those airy-fairy people. I didn't believe that affirmations would work until I looked at the research - there have been some serious medical studies done that showed real results in fields such as mental health, physical health and even smoking.

I will explain how affirmations work, which should help you to realise how beneficial they are. Firstly, your brain can not tell the difference between reality and fantasy. Honestly, it can't. Just consider the following example. Do you remember the last really scary dream you had? Wasn't it terrifying? Didn't the fear feel so real, even for a while after you had woken up? That's because it *was* real for your brain. Your brain honestly thought you had had that experience. You may even have woken up with your heart beating really fast, as your brain sent signals to your body to escape. And it's the same with affirmations.

If you repeat something to yourself often enough, your brain will start to believe it to be true and will respond accordingly. This is why hanging around with negative people is such a drag.

Have you ever had a friend who constantly put you down? I bet you started to believe the things they said about you after a while. And even if the negative comments were not in the least bit true, or if you didn't believe them intellectually, those cruel words may still have had the capacity to make you feel bad deep inside.

That's because the brain works in that funny way, accepting all experiences as valid, whether they are real or truthful or not. What you focus on, you tend to end up experiencing more of. So, keep telling yourself you're a wonderful, happy, positive person and it will improve your ability to make that happen!

Take-aways:

- You are not your behaviours
- You can change
- Knowledge + options + tools = freedom to make the best choices
- Be as consistent as you can. Good choices lead to more good choices
- 'Tell' your brain how you want it to think and behave

"Change starts when someone sees the next step."

- William Drayton

"All meaningful and lasting change starts first in your imagination and then works its way out."

- Albert Einstein

Chapter Seven

It's All in the 'tude

I hope by now you will have started to see what this book is all about. It is only by changing your thinking that you can change your experience. As Shakespeare wrote in Hamlet: "There is nothing either good or bad, but thinking makes it so."

If you're not a fan of the bard, I will translate for you. The same event can be viewed by two different people and experienced entirely differently, depending on their thinking.

As an example, here are some more fictional people for you. Person A and person B are driving along in a car together on the way to a party and it's a stormy evening. The rain is teeming down and the trees by the roadside are blowing about all over the place. Suddenly, a massive tree falls onto the bonnet of the car, crushing it up like a concertina, but hurting neither passenger.

Person A might complain and whine about how the car is wrecked, how they're going to be late for the party, how their insurance premiums will go up. They might think to themselves "Isn't this just typical to happen to someone like me? I'm so unlucky!"

Person B might thank their lucky stars that the tree only hit the car, and not either one of them, and they might feel lucky to be alive. They might feel happy and grateful that they are a lucky person generally.

Now both people experienced exactly the same event, but drew completely different conclusions. And which do you think lives a happier life in general, seeing the good things rather than the bad, the happiness rather than the troubles?

So you might identify more with Person A than Person B at the moment - maybe it's just in your nature to be a pessimist. Don't feel bad about that; as human beings, we are programmed to be on the alert for danger and bad things. It's just part of our survival mechanism that we haven't quite outgrown from the days when everything wanted to eat us.

The good news is, it is no longer necessary to be quite so cynical any longer. And the even better news is that you can actually choose which person you want to be. It is entirely within your power to switch your thinking and your resulting experiences, so that you are no longer a gloomy grump but a positive person who has a better life as a result.

I will tell you a little secret. I used to be an utter pessimist. It was like a skill - I could see the negative in absolutely everything. No matter how many things had gone right in the course of the day, I would focus on the things that had gone wrong. And I would perceive them as much worse than they actually were. And of course, I would then convince myself that I was exactly the sort of person that bad things always happened to. I could cite a massive amount of proof for this 'fact', because, of course, that's what I was always focussing on.

But, one day, I became pretty sick of constantly feeling miserable. The people who were positive seemed to have good things happening to them all the time and appeared to be much luckier and happier than me. So, I decided to become an optimist, by practising looking at the positive side of whatever occurred in my life.

Of course I was extremely sceptical at first, being the good pessimist that I was. But I stuck with it - I already told you I was stubborn, didn't I? And I began to realise that no matter what happened, there was *always* a positive side to it. I could always take some positive element from what, at first, appeared to be an entirely negative situation.

From missing the bus, I could appreciate the fact that I had an extra few minutes waiting in the lovely sunshine. If a party got cancelled, I made the most of it by taking some time to do something nice by myself. Even if something traumatic happened, I saw that it was a chance to strengthen myself, to learn some lessons, and to build up my resilience.

In serious things that would have crippled me with negativity before, I still started to see the positive. When I got into trouble once at work for being careless, I took it as a cue to re-evaluate how much I cared about the job, and I realised I wasn't actually enjoying it any more, quit and got a better job that I loved.

I even looked at my constant relapses positively, realising that they were chances to learn what didn't work, before I was able to finally find the answers. A process of elimination, if you will.

There have been some horrendous and painful experiences, even in sobriety, but I have taken them all as cues to learn and build my own character. If anything bad happens now, I know it will only make me a stronger person when it's over. And focussing on that can make even the most gut-wrenching experiences bearable, and even fruitful.

Positivity is a skill that can be learned - and the people that learn it can make amazing changes in their lives. It does not mean being naïve, and it is not a protective shield against bad things happening. It will not stop other people trying to screw you over, nor stop events not going your way. It doesn't mean your loved ones will live forever, and it doesn't mean you never feel down for no apparent reason at all.

But it does mean that you can recover more quickly from all these things; you can learn from them, rather than wallow in them. And when you can give an event a positive meaning, it becomes helpful to you as a lesson, no matter how dire the circumstances.

Positivity also gives you opportunities - you see ways out of things that negative people just wouldn't consider, because they are too closed-minded. Positivity gives you hope in moments of darkness, and joy in moments of sadness.

It transforms you from an unlucky person into a lucky person, because such things are only matters of perception in the end. There are no lucky or unlucky people in reality - only thinking makes it so. And I hope you can learn to take this attitude to your recovery.

Ask yourself the following questions:

Is it more useful to see yourself as a survivor or a victim?

Is it better to embrace the things you have learned from your difficulties or to curse your whole life?

Is it better to achieve happiness finally or to never even try?

The great thing about this turning-around of your attitude is that no-one can take it away from you; you don't have to rely on other people to make it happen, and you can cultivate it all by yourself. It's free and it doesn't take any special skills or tools.

All it takes is commitment and practice. Everyone can do it if they only choose to, and once you've mastered it, you don't have to do anything else but live that way - and best of all, it is a difference that will translate all across your life.

People are naturally drawn to positive people - they're just nicer to be around. If you're a positive person, you'll find yourself with better relationships, more friends, more fun and more opportunities. All you have to do is learn this skill and embrace it in your life.

Sustained positive thinking can actually work like a dynamo, increasing the likelihood of the brain naturally producing happy thoughts and looking for happiness in future. It's a lovely little trick of the brain that we will explore in more detail later. But, put briefly, focussing on the positives means that your brain will 'learn' to make you happy naturally in future. And if you can learn to see positivity in everything, you can never be a loser.

Nothing is the end of the world

If you're still feeling sceptical, I'd like to share with you a little addendum that helped me enormously when things got tough. No matter how gloomy things might seem sometimes, I want you to remember that nothing is the end of the world.

Now you may have heard that saying so often that it is a mere platitude to you now, without any useful meaning. That's how I used to see it anyway. It was just a thing people said to stop you crying and to make you get on with things.

But think about it properly. Strip that sentence down to what it actually means in regard to your life and everything that happens in it. Nothing that you do, or that anyone else does to you, can cause the world to stop rotating on its axis. However far things have gone wrong, there is always a way back. However much pain I have been in at times, and no matter what a mess I was in, I would always ask myself "Is this going to kill me?" And when I realised it wasn't going to kill me, no matter how bad things seemed, then there was always a chance to change it, a chance to make it better and to move on.

If I look back at some of the things I have gone through, I wonder sometimes how I managed to survive; but I *did* survive and I am here today with a better life than I ever thought possible in those dark days.

Here is an extra special exercise for you to do when things get painful and you feel like it will never end. Save it for the really tough times - I know it will help you out.

Tough Times Exercise

Imagine a line that runs from your past to your future, like a time-line of your life. Most of us have a mental line that we are not always aware of, on which our past memories and future projections are stored.

It will be easy to find where your time-line is - just think of yesterday, or a week ago, and see where that is stored in your memory. Where is it, physically? Is it behind you, or to the left or somewhere else? Where is your sense of the past?

And do the same to locate the future. When you imagine something that's going to happen tomorrow, next week, or next year, where is that 'future memory' stored? Is it in front of you, to your right, or elsewhere?

Now you have a sense of where your time-line is, you can use that when you have hard times to get through in the present.

I'd like you to imagine walking out onto your time-line into the future, wherever that may be for you. Walk out a few weeks or months, or maybe a year, along your time-line, depending on how long you think it might take for you to no longer be deep in this painful problem. Imagine you are now your future self. turn back to look at your 'present self' where you are now in reality. You can either do the walking physically or imagine walking along the time-line in your head.

Your future self will be the person who has got past the pain, overcome the obstacles and grown from the experience. Think about what you, as your future self, might say to that person who is the 'present you' to help them cope with their struggles.

What resources do you think they need that you can now give them? What have you learned as someone who has gone through their particular problem? What might they need to do to resolve it? Send your 'present you' the resources you think they need.

When you can give your 'present you' as many resources, options and comfort as you think they need to bear the pain, come back along your time-line and settle yourself back into the real 'present you'.

Feel that you have all those resources and answers within you now and know that you will be able to cope and go on to be that 'future you' some time soon.

And now on to the more general positivity exercises.

Exercises

You talkin' to me?

A lot of us will be so used to thinking negatively that we even talk to ourselves in a negative way. You know that little voice in your head? The one which tells you things will never work out for you, or that you're stupid or you are always going to fail. That's a by-product of your negative thought patterns.

The thing is, the more you tell yourself negative things, the more you *are* setting yourself up to fail. Have you ever had one of those 'so-called' friends who always puts you down or criticises you? It makes you feel bad, doesn't it? Even if what they are saying is false, or questionable at best. You can make yourself feel bad by talking to yourself in the same way. (A lot of us do that, without realising we are doing it.)

Alternatively, you can decide to change that little voice, challenge it, and finish up with an ally in your head, rather than an enemy.

The first step to change is always awareness. So take these steps to change that self-talk:

   1. When you notice you are saying something negative to yourself, stop and repeat what you just

said out loud, but imagine that you were saying it to a loved one. Change any 'I' statements to 'you' statements or 'we' to 'they' to reflect that change.

2. Now consider deeply how you think your words and tone might affect that loved one. How do you think it might make them feel, saying to them what you have been saying to yourself? Would you feel good about talking to someone in that way? It's not very nice is it?

3. Now we're going to change that voice and take the impact out of those harsh words by changing the voice's qualities. Play around with the tone, first of all. Does making the voice quieter or softer make it a bit easier to deal with?

Maybe you could change the voice to a cartoon character's voice. Could you really make yourself feel so bad if you said "You are a failure" in a Donald Duck voice? How about saying it in a Fred Flintstone voice? Or the voice of a Dalek?

4. Challenge what that voice is saying. Most people never even consider whether that voice is telling them the truth or not. Our negative voices tend to generalise or catastrophise.

So, if you find the voice saying: "I'm no good at anything!" ask yourself the question: "Really? Is there nothing at all I am good at?"

Then come up with a list of things to counter it. How about criticising yourself? - you're certainly good at that. Or how about X, Y and Z? Find examples to prove the voice wrong.

Or if the voice says "You'll never be clever", ask that voice "How do you know?" How about if your voice says: "Nobody likes me!" You can certainly challenge that. Answer it with a list of people who do like you, thank you very much.

5. Once you've started to get the idea that this negative self-talk is unhelpful and can be altered, the next step is to actually change the words the voice says. If you're not quite at the stage yet where you want your inner voice to tell you that you're wonderful all the time, then at least don't let it get away with focusing on the negatives.

Make it constructively critical, rather than downright critical and nasty. So if you make a mistake, don't let your voice get away with saying "You screwed that up, huh? You're always screwing things up!" Instead insist that it say something a bit more helpful and encouraging, such as "Well, that's one mistake I can learn from. What could I do better next time?"

6. Once you've mastered step 5, and that might take some time, then you really should start to turn that mental voice into your own personal cheerleader. I don't mean using it in an egotistical way, but just using it to support you, rather than sabotage you.

Tell yourself "Good job!" when you do things well. If you're feeling a bit overwhelmed, tell yourself "It's OK. You can do it!" How nice does it feel to have a supportive, friendly voice rather than a negative inner critic?

Practising the Positive

This is a practical exercise to get your positivity muscle working. Quite simply, to start with, I would like you to write out some positive ways of looking at the following scenarios. I have done two scenarios for you, with a few examples of positive viewpoints, to give you an idea of how to do it. If you can think of more than one way in which you can draw a positive out of the situation, by all means write more than one positive.

The scenarios towards the end of the list are more serious. If you're stuck, get creative. Think of the learning or positive things you might gain from the scenarios, even if it is only the chance to put things into perspective. Remember, there are *always* positives!

Example 1. All your friends forgot your birthday

Positives:

+ At least it means I won't have to pretend I liked their presents.

+ No-one realises I'm actually a year *older!* No jokes this year about ageing.

Example 2. You lose your passport

Positives:

+ At least that god-awful passport photo of me with that weird 80s hairdo is never going to be seen again.

+ This will teach me to store my belongings in a safe place.

Your turn!

1. You forget your keys
2. You lose your wallet
3. You fail an exam
4. Your pet budgie dies
5. You miss the bus
6. You miss a dental appointment
7. You spill a glass of water on yourself

8. The supermarket has run out of bread
9. You forget your friend's birthday
10. Someone bumps into you
11. You rip your favourite jeans
12. It's raining
13. Someone calls you fat, ugly or stupid
14. You missed the last post
15. Your boss criticises your work
16. You break your ankle
17. Your uncle dies
18. You have to move house
19. Your other half breaks up with you
20. You're late for a job interview

Take-aways:

- Nothing is the end of the world - you will survive even the most painful experiences
- There is no 'fixed' good and bad, only perspective
- You can choose to see things however you want to see them
- You can train yourself to be a positive person, which will make you happier

"A pessimist sees the difficulty in every opportunity; an optimist sees the opportunity in every difficulty."

- Winston Churchill

Chapter Eight

Well I'm Pretty Good at Robbing Banks...

I used to work on an addiction aftercare team, helping people who were coming out of rehab to get back into education, training and employment.

Many of my clients were ex-offenders, having spent some time in jail - or narrowly avoided it. I used to help them write and revise their CVs. And do you know, not one of them put on their CVs under 'Skills': "Pretty good at robbing banks"? And yet some of them were very good at it!

A humorous point, but a serious message. Even when I see that people who have given up drinking and drugging have made some kind of begrudging peace with the past, often they are not wholly convinced by their own attempts at closure.

Well, what if you looked at it another way? What if you celebrated the things that having had your problem has given you? I bet you have never even considered doing that.

We all accept that we are, to a certain extent, products of where we have been, what we have done, experienced and undergone - but we only ever take the bad elements of that, rather than reflecting on all the good things that we've learned and added to ourselves precisely because of our past.

Some recovering addicts who choose to work in the field of addiction recovery have the right idea, in that they know that their knowledge of addiction and addicts is second to none, and they try to use that for good ends. That's really cool, but not everyone wants to go and work in the addiction or social care field.

And anyway, we can take it a step further. Rather than just looking at what you know about addiction, why not look at *everything* that having had your problem has given you, from the extra qualities you might never have had if you hadn't faced addiction issues, to the skills that you have picked up along the way. Look at your experiences and see what they have taught you about yourself and others. Consider what 'transferable skills' you might have, as they term it in the world of work.

I don't mean you have to write them all out on a real CV and send it off to the Job Centre, but just be fully aware of them, appreciate them, celebrate them and the unique person they have made you into. Considering things in this way might feel a little strange at first, as you've probably spent a lot of your life cursing your addiction. But, honestly, you're missing out if you only see the negative things it has brought.

I have come to the point now where I realise that my addiction has given me more than it has ever taken from me. Please read that last sentence again; I truly mean it.

When I was born, if I could have had a choice of lives, I would never, ever have chosen mine, or the path I went down. Of course I wouldn't. If someone had laid out all the choices before me and said, "Well you could become a teacher, a doctor, a builder, a shopkeeper or an alcoholic", I don't think I ever would have said "Hmmm, alcoholism sounds interesting..."

But now that I have come out on the other side, I see the wonderful things that have been given to me, precisely because of what my life eventually turned out like. Precisely *because* of the alcoholic life I led.

We'll move onto gratitude a bit later, as there is a lot more to say about that; but for the moment, let's just focus on what you might not have recognised yet as gifts that you have got from your problems. Sometimes we don't see it, or are so wrapped up in the hurt and the horribleness, that it's too hard to see the bright side. But it is there to see, if you only choose to see it.

So let's start with me - you already know a bit about some of my less-than-pleasant life experiences, but how can I possibly see the good in them? What qualities and skills have they given me?

Here is my 'Alkie CV' and on it I have listed some of the qualities and skills that I have developed as a direct result of my alcoholism and where it led me:

Empathy:

If I can't empathise then I don't know who can. I know what real suffering is because I have been there, so I can feel others' pain. I truly care about people when they are in difficulties.

Ingenuity:

It would have taken a genius to discover where I'd hidden my alcohol all over the house. Much to my annoyance, I even managed to outwit *myself* with my hiding places on some occasions. Over the years I've heard some beauties from other addicts about where they concealed their stash. From hiding bottles in the toilet cistern or burying them in the garden, to storing neat vodka in a vase, as if it was water. Geniuses, we are. Utter geniuses.

Non-judgementalness:

I have met all sorts of people on my travels, and realise that everyone has a story to tell and that you can't judge a book by its cover, nor a person without knowing their life story.

Determination:

I think this goes for all of us without saying. Only bloody-minded sheer determination to drink kept me going sometimes. I have staggered to the shop to buy a bottle when I was in full withdrawal and could barely walk, just because I needed it so badly. And in the end I was so determined to beat all my problems, that no matter how many times I failed, I kept trying. I turned that determination into the drive to start my own business, and hey presto, I'm now using it for good.

Communication:

I have had to be around so many different types of people that I have learnt to communicate on many levels. From drug dealers to police officers, I had to move from one communication style to another seamlessly to stay out of trouble.

Persuasion:

See police officers

Tactfulness:

See drug dealers. You can't be tactless when talking to some of them. You know who I mean.

Sense of humour:

My sense of humour has definitely improved because of my problems. It was forced onto me by the times when I just had to laugh or I would cry instead. And that willingness to see the funny side, even in adversity, has stuck with me ever since. I know a lot of recovering addicts like that.

Creativity:

See police officers again. You have to be creative to get yourself out of scrapes. I often joke about the massive powerhouse that addicts could be in government or politics, with their capacity to be 'creative'.

Flexibility:

I was an accommodating alcoholic, taking changes in my stride. I did anything and everything in order to be able to drink, including moving house more times than I care to remember and sleeping on more sofas than I can count, switching between relationships seamlessly, and making new 'friends' when I'd pissed off all my old ones. That's *some* flexibility.

Strength:

I expect to see this on all of your CVs. All of us have strength in abundance. You have to possess a reservoir of strength, firstly to be able to live as an addict without throwing yourself off a bridge, and secondly to go through the whole process of recovery. It is the hardest thing I have ever done in my life and I'm frigging strong to have done it. And so are you.

Problem-solving:

I got myself into so many corners, but for the most part I managed to get out of them in one way or another. You've got to have some darn good problem-solving skills to get out of some of the situations that I got myself into - and I'm sure it's a similar case with you.

Resilience:

You don't get over being a Relapse Queen without the ability to bounce back. I would not be here now if I wasn't made of such durable stuff.

My ability to give to others:

My whole life wrapped up in a box, with or without a pretty pink bow, was a gift that has allowed me to give so much to others. Even during my illness, I always had a heart within me that just wanted to help and remove suffering. Well, as a product of all my new qualities, experiences and skills, I am now able to fulfil that dream as a Recovery Coach. This is surely the coolest one of all. Pretty neat, huh?

Exercises

My Addiction CV

Write out your own alkie or druggie CV. Don't skimp on anything. Look at all your experiences honestly and squeeze every drop of meaning and positivity out of them. Figure out all the qualities you now possess as a result of your journey. It's there - all you have to do is choose to see it.

Sliding Doors

For anyone who has not seen the 1998 film *Sliding Doors*, it is basically about how the choices that we make can change our lives. One decision can alter the course of our entire lives, even if it seemed like a minute and trivial decision at the time. In the movie, the central character's fate hinges on whether or not she manages to catch an underground train, and the film follows how her life would have unfolded if she did, or if she did not, manage to make the train on time, in two parallel stories.

A lot of the differences in her life stem from who she does, and doesn't, end up meeting along the way, as a result of missing or catching the train, and the opportunities and discoveries that ensue from that one, single incident.

Now the point of the following exercise is not to focus on the might-have-beens - let's be clear about that. You might believe that you have had fewer opportunities as a result of being caught in the trap of addiction. It is easy enough to find evidence for that if you want to, because we often focus on failures in our lives, and on what has gone wrong.

But how about focussing on the unique opportunities you *have* had, ones that are maybe not available to the person who has lived a fairly normal, average life. The things that have happened to you that are not as likely to have happened if you had not had such a chaotic and random life.

I'd like you to take some time to look at the people and experiences you have been *lucky* to have had come into your life as a result of your addiction. Furthermore, explore things that you do not believe you might ever have had if you had not been an alcoholic or a drug addict, with all that this kind of existence entails.

For example, if I had never had my addiction, I would never have met two of the most inspiring people I have ever encountered. One of whom was my old addictions counsellor. I met him when I was still actively drinking. He was a heroin addict in recovery and happens to be one of the people along the way who has stuck in my mind, inspired me, and given me hope. If I had never got so bad that I had to go for counselling, I would never have had this wonderful source of inspiration in my life.

The second was actually a person who was a source of great misery for me. He was also a recovering drug addict and an alcoholic, and he had set up his own project for people who had experienced difficult lives, to enable them go to university. It was this man with whom I compared myself when I first went sober and was struggling to feel recovered. It was that very painful comparison which contributed to my sense that I couldn't carry on in the way that I was, and that I had to find different answers.

In a similar vein, my addiction, and trying to beat, it has also given me the opportunity to learn about myself, to take great strides in educating myself about life and the best way to live it. I've had to look at my flaws and inadequacies, and by doing so I've had the chance to become a much better and happier person.

Another great example from my own life actually involves my relationship with my parents now and their relationship with each other. While my parents are great people and always have been, I genuinely do not think we would be as close as we are now if I had never had any problems in my life.

My parents got divorced when I was a child and while I always maintained contact with both of them and had them in my life, the relationship I have with them now is incredible. After they got divorced and before I became seriously ill, they would be civil to each other but nothing more than that. When things took a turn for the worse with me, they were forced to come together to try and help me. And they ended up getting remarried roughly fifteen years after they got divorced. I am convinced that this would never have happened if I had never become ill.

On an individual basis, I have seen my parents grow as people because of my problems. My dad, in particular, has told me that his experiences with me have made him a better person. He has learnt to be more tolerant, more patient, more forgiving and to be less judgemental of others who may be having problems or mental health issues. Who knows if that would have happened had my experience of addiction not given him such a great, and very steep, learning curve.

In fact, some of the most memorable shifts in our relationship occurred when I was at my very worst, when I was struggling so much. Some of my most difficult and painful times have inspired some of the greatest insights between us and have produced the most touching moments of all.

My friends, too, have shown themselves and their true colours because of my illness. Not very many people get to test their friendships to such extremes as I have. Having accompanied me through my addiction, I learnt which friends were those who would never let me down, and who accepted me even when I screwed up. And those truly are friends worth having. And because of my problems, I know who they are and I value them. I don't have any 'false friends' because they all scarpered as soon as times got tough.

I have also been fortunate enough to experience true kindness on another level from that which we are used to in 'normal' day-to-day life. I have experienced the kindness of complete strangers trying to help me when I had got myself into some mess or another. If it hadn't been for my addiction, I might never have been able to see the beautiful humanity that exists all around us, and that sometimes shows up for us when we really need it.

So now it is your turn to truly appreciate the positive opportunities, the experiences and the people that have shown up in your life as a result of your addiction. You may or may not have had the same experiences that I had with your own family, but you will have had equally valid, important and positive experiences in your life - both as a result of your recovery and as a direct result of your addiction.

Who came out of the woodwork to support you and proved to you that they are a true friend? Who have you met as a direct result of your addiction? What positive experiences and opportunities have you had as a direct result of having such a screwed-up past? What magical moments might never have happened if you hadn't had the life you have had? Who have *you* touched or taught, through your illness?

Explore this for as long as you like, but make sure you come up with some seriously robust and gratifying things that you have got as a direct result of your past, and the choices you made in it.

Take-aways:

- Your addiction has given you many unique skills and qualities - acknowledge them
- Your addiction has given you opportunities you might never have had
- You have better skills in some areas than people who have never lived such a difficult life

> "Two roads diverged in a wood, and I -
> I took the one less travelled by,
> And that has made all the difference."
>
> - Robert Frost

Chapter Nine

The Bacon Buttie of Contentment

I was sitting down the other night to have dinner in my kitchen after a long, arduous day. I decided on the spur of the moment that I fancied a bacon sandwich. Yes, for dinner - it's not against the law you know. So, I popped my shoes on, briskly walked to the shops and bought the bread, the bacon and, of course, the crowning glory - ketchup.

Now, as I said, it had been a long day and my feet were a bit sore, I was quite tired, it was raining and dark. I felt myself sighing a little as I gathered up my shopping and proceeded to go home.

And then I stopped and thought to myself "Why am I sighing? I've just gone out to the shops and got everything I need, and now I'm going home to make a delicious bacon buttie. How lovely!" (For anyone who isn't familiar with a buttie, it's a Northern English term for a rudimentary and indulgent sandwich, such as one filled with oodles of butter, bacon and sauce. Why, what did you think it was?)

As I walked home with my groceries, I felt extremely grateful that I could give myself this simple treat. When I looked back to my ill days, I saw that none of this would have been possible back then. For a start, my anxiety was so great that it would have taken me half a day to persuade myself to leave the house.

There were no spur-of-the-moment treats in those days, unless I was drunk. And then, if I was drinking, would I have even bothered with eating at all? Probably not. But if I had been in a position where I had to go to the shops, there would have been a whole drama involved, just to get something that I needed.

Depending on whether I was drunk or in withdrawal, I might not have been in a state where I was able to walk properly. And even if I managed to get to the shops, more than once I had my card declined due to being out of cash, or due to my inability to type in the correct PIN number.

And so, no matter how tired and achy I felt, my experience that day was one hundred times better than if I had still been in the madness of drinking. And that thought gave me a little thrill, a feeling of joy deep inside my body.

"So, what?" you say? "Don't 'normal' people go to the shops all the time, get on with life just like that and don't make a song and dance about it?" Absolutely, but that's just the point. We recovering addicts can have a deep appreciation of those things that people who have never had such problems just don't have.

If I am having a crappy day and I'm walking down the street, I have the luxury of comparing it with those days when I was agoraphobic, drunk or in withdrawal, and I can truly appreciate how lucky and liberated I am now. Yes, just walking down the street, unafraid and sober, is a miracle and a blessing for me.

While having a horrible past means that we have experienced horrible things, it also provides us with a sharp contrast to what other people consider 'normal' and mundane. Normal people don't usually 'get' that every seemingly humdrum experience can be a joy. We do, because we can compare it with where we were.

It is all about perception again. My difficult and awful life has given me the opportunity to see the magic in going to the corner shop and buying some groceries. If I ever see it as a chore, I can just turn that around quite easily and see it as a blessing. Normal people don't have that! They just see it as a chore.

My friends sometimes think I'm crazy when I talk about how light and lovely I feel when I do something like that on the spur of the moment; what deep happiness I feel from something as simple as that. But

I'm not crazy - I just have a deep, dark experience to compare it with. And from that context, I can take great joy in the contrast.

This wonderful feeling of gratitude, gained from a sense of perspective, is also apparent when I look at all the crazy things I did in the past. Now if you told most people a story of something that happened to you while you were drinking, they wouldn't appreciate it in the same way that we addicts do.

If I told one of my 'normal' friends about getting my mother's house raided for drugs and being arrested in front of my family, they would probably be horrified. But we recovering addicts have the ability to laugh at something like that. It was quite funny, actually, now I look back on it.

It was a trio of plain clothes policemen who came knocking at the door early on a Saturday morning. When my mum opened the door, one of them stuck his foot in the door and held up a warrant. Of course my mum, completely unused to having Search Warrants thrust in her face, thought that they were Jehovah's Witnesses, brandishing the latest issue of *Watchtower*, and she told them "Sorry, we're Zen Buddhists" to try and get rid of them! We weren't as it happens, but my mum's ingenious like that.

At the time, none of this was funny at all, of course, having my poor mum put through this ordeal. But this is the beauty of recovery; we can take laughter from pain. Even my mum jokes about it with me, now that I'm making her proud rather than worried.

What a gift - to be able to take joy from one of the most painful and awful moments of our lives. That is another thing that we addicts have the edge on, compared to most people, and it is something for which we should be truly grateful.

So when I got home that night, ready to make my bacon buttie, as I undertook all the little processes involved in making it, I considered whether or not I would have been able to do those specific things before, when I was ill. And for most of them, the answer was "no". To start with, if I was not in a good space, I would avoid the kitchen entirely, in case someone came in and saw me or I would have to talk to them.

And I did utterly neglect my eating habits when I was drinking. I would either not eat properly for days or I'd be hung-over and binging on junk just to fill my stomach and to try to stop the nausea. And of course, it was never easy for me to eat in front of people, because of my anxiety disorder, so I often went without. I never really enjoyed food in the proper way before I got sober.

As I sat there, indulging in this wonderful bacon sandwich, I realised how lucky I am in all aspects of my life. And while there are people who are better off than me and worse off than me, I am able to fully appreciate whatever I do have, no matter how big or small it is. A spontaneous evening bacon buttie might not mean a lot to most people, but to me it represented everything that was good about my life.

In many ways, my life is better than a lot of other people's, simply because I have the clarity to see all the good in everything I have, and am capable of, these days. I take nothing for granted and I am grateful for everything. More on that later. In the meantime, it is time for you to develop your gratitude even further with the following exercises.

Exercises

Let's do the Time-warp Again

In order to appreciate what you have fully, I want you to do a time-travelling exercise.

What is your sobriety date and how long have you been sober? Now I want you to go back in time before your sobriety date. Travel back the same amount of time that you have been sober for - so if your sobriety date is the

1st June 2010 and you've been sober for two years and one month, go back two years and one month before that, to 1st May 2008.

Now I want you to look at your life then. How would you have introduced yourself to a stranger then, if you were being honest? What could you tell them about yourself?

Here is a list of questions to guide you:

- Who did you have in your life?
- What were you doing?
- Where did you live?
- Were you working?
- What did you do in your spare time?
- Were you healthy?
- Did you have money?
- Were you in a relationship?
- What was your life like?
- What did you feel like?
- What were your dreams then?

And then come forward to the present day and do the same summary of yourself, asking yourself the same questions.

And then compare the two. Don't you have an immense amount of happiness when you look at where you are now as opposed to where you were back then?

Make the Ordinary Extraordinary

The next time you have a task to do that you think is fairly mundane in nature, I'd like you to go through it and appreciate every little bit of it in a way you've never appreciated it before.

Choose something that you would usually think of as boring, or a bit of a drag, to do. Whether it is ironing, washing the dishes, sorting through the laundry, or collecting the kids from school. Or even making a sandwich - or making the bed.

Fully appreciate the experience in a way that you've never done before, paying attention to all your senses and looking at it with an air of curiosity and gratitude. Really go into the minutiae to benefit from this exercise the most.

For example, say you had chosen to look at and fully appreciate the task of washing the dishes - this is how I would do this exercise: First, feel grateful that you have time to do the washing up and be grateful for having washing-up to do, as it means you've eaten something nice, I hope. Then as you start to run the water, listen to it gently trickling or gushing from the tap. Appreciate the fact that you have warm, running water and feel it rushing all over your hands. Does it tickle a bit? Is it soothing or comforting in some way? Then appreciate the washing up liquid with its lovely lemony aroma. Appreciate all the subtle accents in that lovely smell.

Then notice how the bubbles sparkle prettily as they form in the water, and how the soapy bubbles feel on your hands. Then notice how lovely and clean the dishes are becoming, how perfectly the washing up liquid is suited to its task, and how shiny and sparkly the plates and cutlery are after you've cleaned them. Then look at the job you've done, congratulating yourself on having achieved something else today and knowing that next time you need a plate, there'll be a nice clean one just sitting there waiting for you to use.

That was a condensed version - I am sure you can come up with a lot of other lovely things about your own experience. Go and try it now. Pick anything you like. If you can make washing the dishes a bit more fun, think of how you could use this for other even more interesting tasks and activities.

I don't go around celebrating every little thing I do these days, but this is a great exercise to come back to if you're feeling down in the dumps. And any time you do something new that you've never done before sober, celebrate or acknowledge that, too. Be grateful, and you will always be happy.

Take-aways:

- You are luckier than the average person
- You can appreciate things so much more than you would if you had never had problems
- Little things can feel magical
- Gratitude can make you feel happy even in the most mundane of circumstances

"We can only appreciate the miracle of a sunrise if we have waited in the darkness."

\- Author Unknown

Chapter Ten

Like a One-eyed Unicorn

Following on from the last chapter, I'd just like to speak a bit more about gratitude, because it is a very powerful thing. You may think you've heard some of the gratitude stuff before, but I would like you to look at it in a slightly different light. We're going to take a multi-dimensional approach here and be grateful in new ways.

Now some of you may have been asked to write a gratitude list before - and there are a whole number of things you might have put on it. From being grateful for being alive, to being grateful for having your family, or your cat or dog, to being grateful that you have a roof over your head. I would hope that you always have at the top of your list: "I am grateful for being clean and sober". And so you should. But have you ever thought about what that truly means? How deeply lucky you are to be sober at all?

There are currently about 140 million alcoholics in the world and around 15.3 million people with drug dependency problems, according to the World Health Organisation. And I am sure that number is growing.

Studies on recovery from alcohol and drug addiction are sadly flawed, because the results are difficult to quantify. After all, who here has not had a relapse? You're very fortunate if you have not had one - or several. I managed to go sober for around a year before my series of lapses turned into one giant, messy relapse. And yet if you had asked me, I would have said I was in recovery. I never *felt* like I was in recovery, and that's because I wasn't, not like I am today. But if a researcher had happened to put me in a study of alcoholics who were still sober after a year, I would've been counted as recovered, because neither of us knew any better.

The most often cited study regarding recovery in alcoholics is probably the one by the US' National Institute of Alcohol Abuse and Alcoholism (NIAAA) in 2002. The researchers followed a group of 4,422 US adults who met the criteria for alcohol dependence, and then surveyed them after a year[1].

A year on, only 35.9 per cent were considered to be fully recovered, and that included both the 18.2 per cent who had managed to stay abstinent and the 17.7 per cent who were still drinking, but were considered to be 'low-risk' drinkers.

Exactly a quarter of the participants in the study were found to be still *fully* dependent, that's 25 per cent, for people whose maths is as bad as mine.

Some 27.3 per cent of those involved in the study were not considered fully dependent, but still had some symptoms of alcohol dependence or abuse. The final 11.8 per cent were considered to be 'asymptomatic risk drinkers', which meant that they were considered at an elevated risk of relapse as their intake increased.

The authors of the report acknowledged publicly that the survey may have 'inflated' the estimates for recovery, since, among other things, it only included people who had not died from their addiction in the meantime. Indeed, their study mainly covered middle-aged, white males with a college education, who might have had better odds for recovery than some other demographic groups.

It certainly does not take into account the 18 per cent of confirmed alcoholics who commit suicide. In fact, alcohol and drug dependence play a part in more than half of all suicides, with that number extending to 70 per cent in adolescents.

So the study didn't include people who had died from their alcoholism and it only covered the period of a year, not accounting for relapse after that time frame. And the recovery rate within those lean boundaries was *still* only a third.

I cite these statistics not to upset or to depress you, but simply to impress upon you how very lucky you are to be clean and sober, and working on recovery, if that's where you are. Up until now, it has been a very difficult place to get to, and an even more difficult thing to sustain. So every day that you remain in recovery is truly a blessed day.

Actually, I believe that one day the recovery rates will become much better, when the stigma of alcoholism and drug addiction is lifted, as more people will be able to admit to their problems and hold their hands up when they're struggling rather than soldier on and ultimately relapse. Fat chance, you say? There will be more on that, and how you can help, towards the end of the book. But historically, addiction has been a bastard to beat. I think we can all agree on that.

And if I have learnt anything from my journey of relapses and frustration, it is that I am doubly grateful to have full, solid recovery and sobriety, rather than just sobriety alone. Sobriety without recovery wasn't a good place. Externally it was great; internally, I was in my own personal hell.

So, if I write out a gratitude list, the top of mine always reads: "I am grateful to be in recovery", right before "I am grateful to be sober".

Gratitude for opportunities

I'm not going to bore you by pointing out again all the things that you should be grateful for having in your life now. You probably know the drill on that one. But have you ever considered being grateful for all the things you *could* have, the opportunities that are open to you now, the huge potential that you have you now that you've stopped drinking or drugging. I have never seen anyone write on a gratitude list "I am grateful for opportunities" or "I am grateful for the future" or "I am grateful for who I can become now", but those are all great products of recovery and sobriety.

We never know exactly what will happen in the future, but once you're clean and sober, all bets are very much back on. Just look at all the things you can achieve now that you would never have had a chance of doing before.

Look at the potential for developing yourself, the possibility of achieving your goals and living your dreams. No matter what your past holds, you're in the same position now as everyone else for achieving those dreams.

Recovering addicts sometimes say to me that their upbringing, or their problems, or their addiction, has stopped them doing many things. That may be true. But then they go on to say that their past is still stopping them even today. I'm not buying that. I'm sympathetic to their point of view, and I know why they feel like that, but it's just plain wrong.

So you missed out on your education? Neither *Microsoft*'s Bill Gates nor *Virgin*'s Sir Richard Branson got any qualifications at school. Neither did the late, great Steve Jobs at *Apple*. Rapper Jay-Z and boxer-cum-celebrity-griller George Foreman are both high school drop-outs as well as billionaires.

Millionaire grumpy-pants Simon Cowell dropped out of school at the age of sixteen to work in a mail-room. Halle Berry never went to college, and neither did Steven Spielberg. There are so many people who have never let a lack of education hold them back. And if what you want to do does require an education, well, go and get one.

Another excuse that I hear sometimes is along the lines of "Yeah, but it's too late" and/or "I'm too old". There are gazillions of examples of people achieving success later in life. In the world of celebrity, Harrison

Ford, was thirty-five before he even "started earning a regular pay-check", in his own words. Stan Lee, creator of *Spiderman*, was forty-three when he began creating his comic-book heroes.

Laura Ingalls Wilder, who wrote the *Little House* books, got them published when she was in her sixties. In fact, lots of writers did not find success until later in life - James Herriot, of *All Creatures Great and Small* fame, was in his fifties when he wrote his first novel. Frank McCourt was even older, at age sixty-six when his first book, *Angela's Ashes*, saw publication.

Samuel L Jackson was the king of tiny bit-part roles until his success in *Pulp Fiction* propelled him to stardom at the age of forty-six - and he's in recovery, by the way. Clarissa Dickson-Wright, of *Two Fat Ladies* fame, is another recovering alcoholic who started achieving later in life.

Colonel Sanders was the ripe old age of sixty-six when he first found success with his *Kentucky Fried Chicken* empire. And this has got to be one of the most admirable of all - Oscar Swahn won an Olympic medal at the grand old age of seventy-two. In fact, Swahn won six medals, including three golds, during his Olympic career, which didn't start until he was already sixty years old.

I am not saying you have to be rich or famous to achieve success, but what I am pointing out is that you are only as limited as you think you are. In order to succeed, you really only need drive, determination, persistence and the ability to work hard. It doesn't matter what your past was like or where you are now.

Whether you want to be a writer or a teacher, a celebrity chef or a musician, a billionaire or someone who's just comfortable - the opportunities are open to you now. I know that I have taken mine, and there are so many more to come, as long as I'm in recovery. And that is why the sentence "I'm grateful for opportunities" is always featured on my gratitude list, and I hope from now on, it will feature on yours, too.

Exercises

The Future's Bright

This exercise is similar to the one in the previous chapter, where I asked you to take yourself back into the past to recall where you were in life before you got clean and sober. I'd like you to do a similar thing, but this time, project into the future.

If you have been sober for a year, look a year into the future. If it's been three years, imagine three years down the line. And answer these questions based on your ideal future situation, now that you know that you have all the opportunities in the world open to you, as much as the next man or woman.

- Who do you have in your life?
- What are you doing?
- Where do you live?
- Are you working - and what do you do?
- What do you do in your spare time?
- How are you maintaining your health?
- Do you have money?
- Are you in a relationship?
- What is your life like?
- What do you feel like?
- What are your next goals now?

Once you've vividly imagined and pictured this wonderful future, I want you to pick one thing you can do *today* to get you closer to your dreams. It can be anything, from the tiny to the huge - just commit to taking one step to start making it possible. For example, if you planned to write a book, that step could be anything from choosing a topic, to buying a notepad, to writing the first chapter, to researching the market. Just make sure you do one thing that will help you to achieve one of the goals in your dream life. And don't read on until you've done it.

Yeah...But...No...But...YEAH!

Are some of you still arguing for your own limitations? OK, I understand that. It can feel difficult to move from a place of desperation and dying, to a place where you can create a vivid and wonderful life.

There will be some things that you feel are still holding you back from doing what you want to, or even daring to think about what you might achieve.

Maybe you've considered something you'd like to do, but you're coming up with a list of excuses about why you can't do it. You won't see them as excuses, of course; you'll truly believe they are valid reasons. But they aren't.

The only reason people do not achieve things in life is because they make excuses as to why they can't.

Astronaut Buzz Aldrin is a recovering alcoholic. Imagine what would have happened if Buzz had said to himself that he couldn't achieve great things because he happened to be an addict. He's still promoting space exploration and achieving great things, even in his 80s.

But I know where you're coming from if you still feel limited, so complete this exercise to help you overcome those excuses.

1. *Label it*

What exactly is it that is causing you to hesitate and believe that you can't achieve the life of your dreams? Put it down in words: Is it fear? Lack of confidence? Lack of money?

2. *Get options*

Very simply, what are you doing to do to resolve this issue? Make a list of all the things you could possibly do to resolve the problem. From seeing a professional to help deal with your fear, to getting an extra job to make some money. Whatever your obstacle, come up with a whole bunch of things you could do to overcome it, discounting nothing.

3. *Make choices*

Choose a few things that you have decided you will do, put them in order of when you will do them, with deadlines for each.

4. *Take action!*

I don't need to explain this too much, I hope. Get out there and start taking steps to resolve your issues. And when you've done that, go back to the previous exercise and start doing what you really want to do.

Take-aways:

- You're one lucky bunny to be in recovery
- You should be grateful that you have a future
- There are no limits to what you can do with your future other than the ones you perceive.
- Follow your dreams

"As we express our gratitude, we must never forget that the highest appreciation is not to utter words, but to live by them."

- John F. Kennedy

Chapter Eleven

Train your Brain Against Relapse

I mentioned briefly in Chapter Seven how sustained positive thinking can work like a dynamo, increasing the likelihood of the brain naturally producing happy thoughts and looking for happiness in the right places in the future.

This mechanism is due to something rather strange and wonderful called 'neuroplasticity'. This is a fairly modern and very exciting scientific discovery. It has been found that the brain's wiring is 'plastic', or changeable, in non-boffin terms. And guess what? The same mechanism that causes you to become addicted to drugs or alcohol is the same thing that can stop you relapsing if you know how to 'work' it.

I will explain to you how the brain works when addicted. You didn't become an alcoholic or an addict the first time you took a drink or drug, did you? You might have liked it, and wanted more, but that utter compulsion to use drink or drugs was not there in the same way as when you came to the end of your addiction and you literally would have walked over hot coals to get to your drink or drug of choice.

That is because, through using drink and drugs, you managed to 'rewire' your brain, reorganising its neural pathways. Neurons are the nerve cells in the brain, by the way, and the neural pathways, or connections between them, are called synapses.

The way that addictive substances work on the brain is that they interfere with the normal 'reward system' mechanism in the brain. With repeated use of addictive drugs, the brain's synapses become physically changed to fit the new usage of that synapse, rather than the natural reward system that we would use when we love, laugh or bond.

This is why addicts find that they need more and more drugs or drink to get a hit, and find less and less satisfaction in normal 'rewards' such as food, sex, sociability and relationships. And that's also one of the reasons why you felt like a fish out of water at parties when you were newly sober. Your brain didn't 'get a hit' as easily from natural highs any more.

Now, it was previously believed that your brain stopped growing in childhood, but thanks to studies in stroke victims, who were able to 'adapt' other parts of their brain to do the jobs of the parts that had been damaged, we now know that your brain is constantly growing and altering its structure.

But your brain doesn't grow haphazardly, or according to some pre-determined blueprint. Actually you can change your brain yourself; because the very thoughts you think, your focus and your decisions, all affect the way that the brain changes and grows.

Amazingly, thought can actually alter the brain's physical structure as well as the way it functions. Over time, you can change the hard-wiring of your brain, making it 'learn' a different way of thinking. Constantly thinking in a particular way will strengthen the appropriate synapses, and so this will result in a new way of behaving for you that becomes like an automatic function as the synapses are reinforced by repetition.

So how does this work in relation to relapse? Well, addiction is characterised by faulty wiring in the brain; it has become that way due to repeated exposure to the addictive substance.

Every time that you had a drug and it gave you a buzz and every time that you had a drink and it cheered you up, you were strengthening and developing that faulty wiring system. We are still not sure why this happens in some people's brains more than in others (it appears to be genetic), but if you are an addict, this is what has happened to your brain.

So, it makes sense that by doing more positive things to give you those rewards that drink and drugs gave you, you will be rewiring your brain the right way. In effect, you're changing the old 'addicted' pattern and normalising your brain function.

Therefore, the more that you use a healthy coping mechanism, the less likely you are to be inclined to relapse, because the right neural pathways are being strengthened, and the faulty ones are becoming less and less active.

This is why positive thinking, increasing your self-esteem, forming friendships and treating yourself to healthy rewards are all great forms of protection against relapsing. You're actually teaching your brain a better way of being.

Having a positive environment will also help you - I'm sure you know what a negative environment does to your thinking and mood. Well, if you can surround yourself with positive sensory experiences, people and situations, you are likely to feel positive emotions more often. This is why I've had to stop listening to Nirvana and Manic Street Preachers quite as much as I used to.

If it's easier, think of the brain like a muscle - you can develop certain parts of it and make them stronger by doing certain exercises.

Your reactions, perceptions, behaviour, thoughts and imagination will all affect the development of your brain 'muscle' - so if you choose to exercise positive choices in these areas, you can go a long way to making your brain work better for you.

I have already experienced the brilliant results of rewiring my own brain, by constantly practising things that break my old patterns. I think I mentioned before how I used to get hideously angry about certain situations. The Incredible Hulk had nothing on me when I really got going. I could hold a grudge like most people hold stubborn belly fat. If someone pissed me off, they would have to stay away from me for the rest of the day, or risk my wrath.

But it was by interrupting that pattern of anger, little by little, that I managed to change that. So, any time I got angry, I would stop and reason with myself. Was this a reasonable way to behave? More often than not, it wasn't. And ultimately, it was making me, and everyone else who dared to step on my toes, unhappy. So I would stop myself, apologise and settle down.

It wasn't easy at all, particularly at first, but the more I did it, the shorter my grudges became. And the earlier I intervened in my own rage-fests, the more effective I was at stopping them short. Now if you break my boundaries, you can expect a short, sharp word, followed by a proper, adult conversation, forgiveness and a hug, more often than not, shortly after.

This mechanism works with any way of thinking or behaving that your brain has learned to do. You can unlearn any bad mental habits or behaviours you have learnt. How cool is that?

Now without arguing about all the different models of addiction, I am pretty sure that most of you realise there is a big psychological element to addiction, as well as a physical one. Studies have shown that genetics and biology also come into play. So, don't go thinking you can just re-train your brain and go back to the drink or drugs. We don't know enough about the other ways that substances can affect the brain to come to a safe conclusion on that one, and there seem to be some permanencies that can't be reversed.

The evidence is that no-one can go back to being un-addicted. If you pick up a drink or drug again, you'll be back to square one. So, don't even go there.

But hopefully, if you embrace the principles in this book, you'll be so addicted to happiness and recovery that you wouldn't even consider going back anyway. That's how I feel most of the time. Even though there are some awful times when something dreadful happens, and I'd just like to take the edge off, I can honestly say 99.9 per cent of the time I'm delighted to be a teetotaller.

Exercises

Rewire your Reactions

Now I know that we addicts can be a stubborn (ahem, I mean determined) lot. So for this exercise I'm going to ask you to be wilful on purpose. Choose one situation in which you know you react or behave negatively, and commit to reacting in a better way for the next two weeks of your life.

You could pick anything - from not getting annoyed at your kids or your partner when they do something that irritates you, to not passing on gossip when you really want to. Or not telling yourself off when you make a simple mistake. And don't just sit there feeling that you want to react but can't - choose a different way of reacting to replace the old behaviour.

So when you screw up, instead of calling yourself stupid, say under your breath "It's OK, I made a mistake." Instead of gossiping, say something positive about someone. Instead of screaming at your loved ones, practise smiling instead, or being calm as you say what is on your mind.

Naturally, I'd like you to do it for more than two weeks to really start to cement the changes, and to apply this to all the negative things you do in your life; but one thing, and two weeks of practising it, is a great place to start changing your habits. And don't give up, as it won't have the desired effect if you do. Commit to doing it even if you don't feel like it - that's the way that it'll become automatic and effortless for you in future.

Balance your Brain

Unfortunately, sometimes our brains are more likely to pick up on negatives rather than positives, particularly if you're naturally a negative thinker. For example, if five people say something nice to you about your appearance, but one person is critical of your shoes, guess which remark will stick in your mind? That's right it'll be the silly person who criticised your choice of footwear. I think this probably goes back to a survival mechanism and is possibly a remnant of our caveman days. But that doesn't mean it can't be changed. So try the following exercise.

At the end of the day, go through all the events that happened in your mind and pick out all the positive things that you can. If your mind automatically starts focussing on the unpleasant memories, that's OK. But before you've finished, make sure you have at least as many positives in mind as negatives.

If you can already do that, then try to make sure you have double the amount of pleasant thoughts as opposed to negative. Keep challenging yourself to think in that way and it will become automatic.

Take-aways:

- Your neural pathways can be changed
- You can make yourself less likely to relapse by correcting your brain chemistry
- Work on giving yourself 'healthy' rewards
- Good habits can be formed to replace bad habits

"First we make our habits, then our habits make us."

- Charles. C. Noble

Chapter Twelve

Excuse me - Would you Kindly Stop Pissing on my Rainbow?

Now as you already know, we addicts are sensitive people. It sometimes doesn't take much to spark off a negative emotion in us, and once we are in that bad emotional state, it is easy for us to start questioning everything and making excuses or picking holes.

Let me tell you a story. In my early sobriety (the second time around, since you asked), I nearly threw it all away because someone stepped on my foot in the supermarket.

That's right, I had battled through horrendous Delirium Tremens, I'd come out the other side and was a few months into sobriety (I hadn't managed a month since my initial relapse) and I nearly chucked it all in and drank because someone happened to stomp on my Skechers with their foot. Not only was I thinking of chucking in my sobriety, I was wondering whether I'd better not just chuck myself under a bus as well for good measure. Yeah, there goes the drama queen again.

To be fair to me, it wasn't just the injury to my foot - it was a combination of a grey sky, me getting wet in the rain because I forgot my umbrella, a bus driver shouting at me and *then* someone having the audacity to step on my foot.

"Where was all your positivity then, Beth?" You might well ask. The thing is that even though I had learned a lot of this stuff already, I have within me a massive capacity for being contrary, for catastrophising, and for feeling a bit hard done by if the circumstances are right (or wrong). I also happen to have Borderline

Personality Disorder, which really doesn't make things any easier. This means that I am extra-prone to losing it when problems start piling up.

I'll tell you what I get most pissed off by - it's when I'm doing all the right things and taking the right steps, but other people don't seem to be! I can't tell you how frustrating I find it when I'm being Little Miss Good and people just carry on in their selfish ways anyway.

The thing to remember here is that you only have the power to control *yourself* and *your* actions and responses - no matter how nice you are, some people are just idiots and a-holes and there is nothing you can do about them.

OK, I don't quite mean that as harshly as it sounds - I actually have a totally tolerant approach to people these days; but when you are first starting out, and struggling with other people's behaviours, it does *seem* like they are idiots and a-holes. Actually, they are only trying to make their way in the world, just as you are, doing the best that they can do.

We all have bad days and bad weeks, and some of us even have bad lives, compared to others; and people who appear antagonistic, careless or malicious are just trying to cope with theirs in their own way. Sometimes other people will get caught up in their 'stuff', which is a shame, but it's just the way life is.

I find myself accepting people these days, with all their foibles, problems and bad attitudes, because I can not let myself get caught up in their negativity. I *must* do my best, no matter what other people are doing, or what is on their agenda.

And yet again your inner voice may have started shouting: "But it's not fair. Why do I have to be all nice and self-improvement-y when other people aren't bothering?" Well the truth is you have to look after your responses and your actions, because if you don't, you won't be in recovery for long. Or even if you remain in recovery, you won't be at peace with yourself.

Non-addicts can quite probably get away with having a bad pattern of thought without it killing them - but addicts are more likely to tear themselves apart with worry, guilt, remorse and negativity. And that sort of thing sends you straight back down the path to becoming an unhappy recovering addict, and that can lead to relapse.

Quite simply, when sometimes we want to rant and rave and chuck it all in, we have to look at what the long-term result of our actions will be. Let's face it, we're not naturally good at this, us addicts. My last two withdrawals were the worst I ever had - and yet why was the penultimate one not the last one? Because I hadn't played the tape forward, as per usual.

When I bought that final bottle of spirits, I never saw the days of agonising withdrawals and shame coming in a week's time, even though I had been there many times before. I only saw the immediate relief from pain and upset. And that is precisely why, as addicts, we have to work on ourselves, whether we like it or not. We can not afford to be complacent about this.

Our short-term thinking and negative outlook will, in all likelihood, get us into serious trouble. That's why it is absolutely vital to stop the onslaught of negativity, or wanting to hit the wall and give up, as *soon* as you see it coming. At first you might find that you only notice you're doing it *after* you've already done it. You'll have gone down in that negative spiral before you had a chance to get yourself out of it.

But as you make a commitment to be aware of every time you do this, it'll become easier and easier to spot. You'll be able to see it coming and to stop it in its tracks.

It's not always easy taking on a whole new way of thinking, so don't beat yourself up if it's tricky at first. Take heart though, as the more you do it, the easier it will become. And once you've been doing it for a while, you will start to do it automatically.

I can safely say that now if anyone happens to shove me on the train, or to give me a cross word, it doesn't pull my whole day down - as long as I make the effort to pull myself up. And that's the best reason of all for sticking to the rules of good and positive recovery - that ultimately it will make you happier overall. And that's the whole point of it, isn't it?

So, when someone insists on pissing all over your rainbow, just remember it's *your* rainbow and it's there to make you happy. So stick with it!

A rather nice secondary benefit of this is that by doing the right thing, we become a role model for others to follow, and our own ripples of positivity can have far-reaching consequences.

It may not seem apparent to you sometimes, because human beings can be selfish, self-absorbed, and they don't always have the resources to respond positively. And people do screw up and make poor choices; but actually you *will* influence others with your own positivity. Maybe the whole world will not change overnight, but you can make a small difference and that can have a big impact overall.

Have you ever heard the story about the starfish? Originally told by Loren Eiseley in *The Star Thrower,* the story has a few versions. Basically, it tells of a man walking on the beach one morning when he comes across another man standing next to the sea and throwing things into it.

As he comes closer, he notices that the man is reaching down to the sand, picking up starfish off the beach, and gently throwing them back into the sea. Intrigued, the first man asks the stranger why he is throwing starfish into the ocean.

"The sun is up, and the tide is going out, and if I do not throw them in, then they will die," the stranger responds.

"But there are miles and miles of beach and starfish all along it," the first man points out. "You can not possibly make a difference."

140

Upon hearing those words, the stranger just carries on. He picks up another starfish and throws it into the sea, saying, "It made a difference to that one."

In some versions of the story, the first man joins him on his mission, too, and so do others who happen to be walking along the beach.

The story has many messages - among them is that it doesn't matter what anyone else thinks, or says, you should still continue to do the right thing. Another lesson is that doing the right thing can sometimes influence others to do the same. And that even if you think you are just making a small difference, the impact can be massive.

It is so important to do what you believe to be right. I hope by now you can see that positivity, making the right choices, and taking action, are all a big part of that, no matter what anyone else's agenda or response.

Exercises

Play the Tape Forward

This is a great exercise to do if you ever feel tempted to cave in and drink or take drugs; but you can use it in any circumstances where you feel like doing something that is probably not the right thing to do.

Essentially, all you will be doing in this exercise is stopping for a moment and imagining what could happen if you indulged in an undesired behaviour, and then comparing that with your possible future if you didn't do the undesired behaviour.

I'd like you to consider both the short-term results and the longer term results, so we're going to look at what might happen tomorrow and over the coming weeks and months, as a result of your decision - and what your life might be like five years down the line.

I'll use the example of drinking to show you how detailed I'd like you to make your investigation of both future paths.

If I were to drink tonight, I could expect:

Tomorrow: Feeling that awful compulsion to drink again, feeling guilty, feeling sad, wondering what I did and who I upset, maybe physically injured or ill, feeling ashamed and regretful. Can't look other people in the eye. I'd have let everyone down.

Next week: Caught up in the trap again. Probably still on a binge or now in withdrawal. Either way, unable to go out. Too ashamed to talk to anyone; physical discomfort and sickness. Maybe ending up in hospital.

Next month: Broke, broken, lost faith in myself. Having to start all over again.

Five years from now: Maybe still relapsing or having returned to drinking. Maybe lost friends, family, work or home. Wasting my life. Or dead.

If I were to abstain from drinking tonight, I could expect:

Tomorrow: No hangover, no compulsion to drink more, a clear head, to get on with whatever I already had planned, feeling strong, guilt-free and proud of my decision. Others proud of me.

Next week and next month: Feeling positive and strong. Still making good progress. Further on in recovery, physically, mentally and emotionally.

Five years from now: The world is my oyster. I could be doing any number of wonderful things now, and all because I chose to do the right thing.

Your turn to do the exercise, comparing what would happen if you chose to cave in to bad behaviours or not.

Vulcanicity

Most of us have been brought up to be reasonably judgemental, even though this sort of attitude can make us resentful, cross and unhappy.

It is another of those short-cuts that we used to use in the caveman days to decide whether someone was an enemy or a friend, and whether a food was likely to be poisonous or not. A lot has changed since then and our world is a wonderfully varied and diverse place. There are all sorts of lovely people, things and experiences we may miss out on if we judge them too quickly and dismiss them. We should not rush to make judgements of things and people all the time. But, of course, we are used to it and so it will take practice to change that automatic reaction.

Here is a great exercise to help you practise keeping an open mind and letting go of judgement. This is a little bit like meditation, but if you don't already meditate, don't let that put you off. Meditation really only means focussing on something.

Find somewhere comfortable to sit, and maybe close your eyes if it helps. And just let your mind wander.

Take a curious attitude. Whatever your mind happens to think of, just let that thought be a thought, and don't make a judgement about it.

Act as if you are an observer of your own brain. Imagine you're a Vulcan, like Mr Spock; an emotionless observer. You can label things as facts or as opinions, when you see them pop up.

If your brain happens to think of something that is a judgemental thought in itself, step back and observe it as a judgement, rather than getting caught up in it.

For example, if you start thinking "Am I doing this right? I bet I'm not!" just step back from that and instead think "I am wondering if I'm doing this right. I appear to be of the opinion that I'm not doing it right."

Do this for just a few minutes the first time you try it. You'll be able to do it for longer periods of time the more you practise.

Yes, it is quite Spock-like. And this is one of those exercises that takes practice to master. But it's well worth practising, as the benefits of it include becoming calmer and being better able to let go of pain and negative emotions. When you can see your automatic judgement for what it is, it is easier to let go of it.

Just a Little Patience

As I mentioned before, most people do not want to be inconsiderate idiots. You may find that difficult to believe, but just look at it this way. When you were drinking or using drugs, did you set out specifically to piss off a load of people? No, I bet you didn't set out to do that. But I'm sure if your using was anything like mine, you will have hurt a lot of people, behaved in some very inconsiderate ways, and angered or upset people all the same. It's not what we wanted to do, and perhaps people called us selfish or wilful, when actually we were addicted. It is easy to judge others and to get the wrong idea about their intentions, but it is also lazy, unfair and leads to unhappiness overall.

This exercise is designed to give you the chance to have compassion and understanding towards other people, instead of being irritated by their behaviour; and to think about some of the various reasons why they might be acting in the way that they are.

Firstly, I want you to identify a word or action that you can use to interrupt yourself whenever you feel you are thinking critical thoughts about someone else, or whenever you feel that you are likely to react to someone else with anger or irritation over some silly, petty issue. It has to be something you can use in the moment; something short and snappy. Some people like to count to three, some simply take a deep breath and others might shout to themselves, inside their head: "Stop!" Choose whatever works for you, as long as it is something that will work after practising it a few times.

So when you encounter someone who is pushing your buttons, as you feel the urge to react beginning, use your interrupting word or action. Then the next step in the process is to think of at least one reason why they might be acting in that way, and then to think of a way that you could treat them with kindness.

For example, if someone pushes past you on the tube, here are some examples of reasons you might consider:

1. Maybe they're late for a job interview
2. Maybe they're late for a hospital appointment
3. Maybe they're anxious or having a bad day
4. Maybe someone pushed into them
5. Maybe they just didn't see you in time

The truth is you can never know most people's reasons for behaving in what appears to be an inconsiderate way. But rest assured, they will usually have some kind of reason, and they are unlikely to have done whatever they did just to ruin your day. What small actions could you take, then, to make the world a better, and more patient, place? I always like to smile, or just to excuse the behaviour with no reaction at all.

And don't think this is about just 'grinning and bearing it' or letting people walk all over you. It isn't at all. It's about having compassion for another person, and choosing not to make the situation worse for them, or for you, by reacting negatively.

Remember, every time you do something negative, it affects you too! Every time you frown or look cross, you're sending messages to your brain telling it to be angry and upset. Smiling actually releases endorphins into the bloodstream, meaning that if you weren't happy before, choosing to smile can cheer you up. So do yourself and others a favour and choose to be patient, compassionate and kind.

Take-aways:

- People are just trying to do the best they can, even if they make mistakes or act badly
- You owe it to yourself and the world to remain positive
- You keep yourself safe by doing the right thing
- Behaving well will make you happier overall

"Be the change you want to see in the world."

- Mahatma Gandhi

Chapter Thirteen

That's an Affirmative, Captain...

While I have emphasised the need for positivity in the previous chapters, a few of you may have started to become a little sceptical, thinking you can't possibly change so dramatically, or not seeing the point of it all. It's OK - that's pretty normal. It may be in your nature by now to be cynical. That's only to be expected, knowing where you have come from. Let me investigate this pattern a little further, and then I'll explain why it is vital for you to work on this element of your thinking.

If you were to ask a recovering alcoholic or drug addict, or even one who is not yet in recovery but is starting to hope for change, or thinking about becoming clean, what do you think they would hope for the most? Why do we want to stop drinking and drug-taking? What would be the point of getting sober?

Most addicts could come up with a whole list of reasons, such as:

- I want to stop letting people down
- I don't want to be ill any more
- I don't want to feel out of control
- I don't want to argue with my family
- I don't want my friends to abandon me
- I don't want my spouse to leave
- I'm worried about losing my job, home or money
- I don't want to go to prison (again)
- I hate lying
- I hate my life
- I hate looking like crap
- I don't want to be a slave to drink/drugs
- I want to stop wasting my life

Do any of those look familiar?

How about these?

- I want to be responsible
- I want to show up for life and be there for other people
- I want to be healthy
- I want to be in control of my actions and responses
- I want to have a great family life
- I want to have strong friendships
- I want to have a loving and stable relationship with my partner
- I want a secure and happy career and home
- I want to be free and law-abiding
- I want to live my life in a truthful way
- I want to love my life and every part of it
- I want to look my best and be proud of my appearance
- I want to be in control and free
- I want to build an incredible life

Now most addicts will identify fully with the first list, but they may find the second list a little alien. Of course you may want all of those things, but you're more likely to verbalise your wishes in the terms stated on the first list. You are more likely to state what you wish to avoid, rather than what you wish to have. All I have done in the second list is to turn the statements from negative 'aversive' statements to positive ones. And I'll tell you why that's important.

As I told you before, the brain can be a funny thing. The first thing you should know is that the brain doesn't process negatives very well. I'll give you an example. *Don't* think of a purple pony. Right, I said *don't*, but the first thing you did was to think of a purple pony. I know you did, because that is the way our minds work.

Your brain has to formulate a picture of what you're talking about before it has time to process the instruction *not* to think about it. So, in that way, you're actually focussing on the very thing you want to avoid. And I'll tell you why that's a bad thing. Whatever you focus on, you tend to get more of.

I'll give you an example. I broke my ankle a few summers ago (no, I wasn't drunk this time) and I ended up on crutches for about six months. During the time when I was hobbling around on crutches, I noticed a lot of other people on crutches. "How funny," I thought. "Lots of people must have accidents at this time of year!" But of course the accident rate in London didn't happen to go up at exactly the same time that I broke my ankle. In fact, there were no more people in London on crutches than at any other time. I was just *noticing* them more. Why? Because I was focussing on my own crutches. Crutches were my world, so that's what I saw wherever I went.

The same thing happened the first time I got sober. I noticed alcohol everywhere! Because I was so desperately focussed on *not* thinking about alcohol (remember how the brain is with negatives), I ended up seeing it all over the place.

I would notice discarded cans by the side of the road. Alcohol advertising would jump out at me from bus shelters. I would be the one to clock the guy sipping something out of a paper bag on the street, whom no-one else had spotted. I'm sure you can recall similar experiences in your own life, where once something was at the forefront of your mind, you seemed to notice it everywhere you went.

Don't start cursing your brain for this strange anomaly just yet - the main purpose of this function is probably survival-based. For example, if you were running around in caveman times feeling hungry and thinking about food, it would have been jolly useful to have our brain focussing on food for us, helping us to spot the berries, plants and woolly mammoths.

And once we know that our brain works in this particular way, we can use that knowledge to improve our lives. Imagine you wanted to find a new partner. Instead of saying to yourself, "God, I hope I don't end up with another loser/emotional pygmy/selfish so-and-so..." you could focus on the qualities you really want in a partner.

And the same goes for your sobriety. Instead of focussing on the things you want to avoid by getting clean and sober, think about all the things you will *get*. While it is much more likely that you *will* get those things by focussing on them, there is another reason why it is very important for us recovering addicts to have positive motivations rather than negative ones.

Initially, the first list of statements, of what you want to avoid by getting clean and sober, might appear more powerful to you than the second list, especially if you are new to sobriety.

After all, when we were first motivated to get sober it may have been a matter of life or death for us, or simply a matter of trying to avoid losing all that we loved. Those are very powerful motivations at the beginning. But what about a few months down the line when you're feeling better physically and mentally, and your life is starting to improve? When your partner is no longer threatening to leave you every night, and your boss has a new-found respect for you. You know, basically, when you're doing OK. Well, you're not being motivated by those massive pitfalls that you wanted to avoid any more, are you? You've side-stepped them, hopefully, and life is kind of dandy. And well, maybe you could have a drink or drug to celebrate...

Do you see where the danger lies here? When you've already *achieved* the avoidance of the awful stuff, the motivation to *stay* sober is no longer there in such a compelling way. Now that the bruises have healed, relationships have improved, you're feeling a bit better, and have become more reliable, you are less desperate to stay sober.

So what do you need to do? You need to create a compelling reason to *stay* sober and that can really only be done by creating things to constantly work towards rather than to move away from. In my own experience, the more amazing you can make your dreams, the more likely you are to *want* to work on them. And then you've got to stay sober in order to achieve them.

And when I say the more amazing your dreams, the better chance you have of continually motivating yourself to stay sober, do not mistake this for meaning that your dreams have to be wild, crazy, and practically unachievable. All I mean by 'amazing dreams' is that they are things that would be absolutely 10/10 wonderful for you to have, things you would be so proud of achieving, or happy about having or doing, that you just *have* to work towards them. Goals and dreams that put a big old smile on your face just thinking about them.

Do not set yourself up for failure by having a dream such as "I want to win the lottery" or "I want to marry a film star." Have dreams that may be big, but if you really worked for them, you could achieve them.

For example, part of my dream involved setting up my own business, spreading the recovery message through my work, and helping as many people as possible to live amazing lives. I knew I could achieve none of that without my sobriety. In fact me being sober is clearly integral to my mission.

So, I want you to write out some of the best motivators imaginable for staying sober. The big dreams that you can look forward to achieving in recovery. If you start to write small, crummy dreams, I will tell you off, and tell you to go and read about limitations again, in Chapter Ten.

But if you're ready to start setting big, exciting, achievable goals, then get on with the exercises on the following page.

Exercises

DREAM BIG!

Here are a few inspiring questions I want you to answer in order to help you to find your dreams. Don't blast through the questions in a rush. Instead, take your time. Really think about your answers. You can even do this exercise over a few days if you like. Sit down for a session with a big notepad, and then come back to the list when you've slept on it. This is an important step in building your future.

*   What do you want more of in your life?
*   If you knew you couldn't fail, what would you do?
*   What job would make you so happy that you'd do it for free?
*   What is your most important value and how would you like to show it in your life?
*   If there was a miracle overnight and your life was transformed what would that look like?
*   What is the thing you'd most like to achieve in life?
*   What would make your life meaningful?
*   What would you like your legacy to the world to be?
*   What would you have to do to know you could die with no regrets?
*   What dream makes you smile just thinking about it?
*   How do you want to show that your life was important?
*   What would get you out of bed every morning, even if it was stormy, because you just want to do it so badly?
*   What do you want to be written on your epitaph?

Remember when you are dreaming, that it's all very well to have dreams which include other people, but do *not* make your dreams completely contingent upon anyone else. All of these things must be within *your* power to achieve. It is fine to dream about marrying your current partner or having children with them, but do not make your dream *all* about that. Because in the end, you can not control other people's destinies. What they want, and ultimately what they do, is not down to you. Accept that they might not be part of your dream - if it was meant to be, then it will happen; but if not, then it was never yours to dream about.

Categorise your dreams into two parts - the first should be all the things that you want to achieve and which you can do through your own agency. You may need favours or good fortune along the way, but ultimately if you work hard enough, they are things that you can get done. And then, anything that falls under the heading of something you may have no ultimate control over, put in a second 'nice to have' category.

Now you should have formed some idea of what your dream life would be. You should have a vision that inspires you, and that makes you desperately want to live an amazing, clean and sober existence, so that you can achieve it.

Sound Vision

OK here is where the real magic starts to happen. There is no point in having grand dreams and designs unless you plan to do something about them.

So here is where you are going to create some kind of framework for achieving your dreams, turning that vision into something solid and real.

For dreams to be achieved, it is necessary to break them down into a series of smaller goals. And each goal has to be specific and solid so that you can create an action plan around it. Otherwise, how would you know where to start?

So, for your dreams above, break them up into smaller goals that you will need to meet to achieve your ultimate vision. You might want to do this like a spider diagram, where your dream is in the centre, and the goals are all of the legs coming off it.

Now for each goal, you need to make it realistic and achievable by setting it out according to the following rules. It needs to be very specific, with a deadline, with all the steps outlined of how you plan to achieve it. So, if your dream was to become a famous author, you might have mini-goals, such as outlining the book, writing each chapter, obtaining an agent etc.

And for each of those goals, list under it, very specifically, what you are prepared to do, and by when. There is no point writing out stuff that you know you won't do - or that you can't possibly achieve. For example, if you have to get an agent, be aware that this could take a number of months, so don't give yourself a two-week deadline.

Remember to be as specific as you can about your goals, so that you'll know when you've achieved them. Now is not the time for airy-fairyness. It's time to get solid, specific and set on actually achieving what you want to.

Take-aways:

- Your brain doesn't process negatives properly
- Your brain focuses on whatever you think about
- State your motivations in the positive
- Give yourself a reason not just to get clean and sober, but to stay clean and sober
- Dream big!

"I forgive myself for having believed for so long that...I was never good enough to have, get, be what I wanted."

- Ceanne DeRohan

"Make no little plans; they have no magic to stir men's blood...Make big plans, aim high in hope and work."

- Daniel H. Burnham

Chapter Fourteen

No Need for Lycra

OK I don't want to scare you off with the word 'transcendental'. There, I've said it now and I'm not going to take it back. Unfortunately, this word has been misappropriated in some ways, and now if someone says the word 'transcendental', most people start rolling their eyes and expect you to start chanting and putting candles on the floor. Or maybe they're worried you'll get out the Lycra and start doing a bit of Yoga. "Come on," you're thinking. "Don't start telling me about angels, light energy and rainbows." Or maybe that's just me.

Well anyway, don't worry, that's not what the word really means.

Tran·scen·den·tal as defined in the dictionary can have the meanings below:

1. transcendent, surpassing, or superior
2. being beyond ordinary or common experience, thought, or belief
3. beyond the contingent and accidental in human experience, but not beyond all human knowledge

All that 'transcendental' means is looking at things from a perspective that gives more meaning to things than you might ordinarily ascribe to them. Phew, not quite as scary as all that was it? And there's no need for Lycra. It's a winner all round.

What I am asking you to do is to think beyond how you might have already considered your experience of things. In essence, to think about your life in terms of more than just events that have happened or are going to happen, but to consider what their happening might have been *for.* A deeper reason, if you like.

Do you believe you are here for a reason? Do you believe that your experiences have happened to you for a reason? In this book, we have gone through a lot of the positive traits that having had a hard life can give you. We know about the joys of recovery, the gratitude that we can now have for our sobriety and our lives. We know that, if we choose to, in recovery we can do some pretty nice and positive things. We know that, as addicts, it's pretty nice to help others out, to give back to other people, and to treat the rest of the world in a nice way; but is there even more to it all than that?

What if you could assign a meaning to your experiences, so that you not only see them in a positive light, and see what they have given you, but perhaps you might even suppose that these things have happened for a damn good reason. Wouldn't that be awesome; if there was a reason for all that suffering? A really amazing and inspiring reason?

I'm not going all religious on you either - I don't care if you're religious, but I'm not. You don't have to be religious, or even spiritual, in the traditional sense, to find deeper meanings in your experiences.

It took me a long time to be happy that I was ever an addict. A lot of my sobriety was ruined by me thinking about how awful it was that some of us were subject to such terrible lives, and really feeling rather down about that. And even when I could see the skills and qualities that having my addiction had given me, I still felt like I was unlucky.

I thought "Fine, let's make the best of this, think positively and count my blessings." And that was good, and certainly better than feeling like I had done nothing but waste my life all those years; but it still left me somewhat puzzled as to why these bad things had happened to me. Or why they have to happen to anyone else in the world.

As I said, I am not a religious person at all - and I count myself as both a philosophical and rational person, generally. I have always been bothered by the apparent cruelty and suffering in the world, and I used to often question why the human race and our planet are the way they are.

So, although I was much happier thinking of my experiences in a positive way, I was still left slightly unsatisfied by doing that, and I felt that there was a piece of the puzzle still missing.

It wasn't enough for me to have learned a little something from the fact that I had had my life ravaged by addiction and other mental health problems. The learning there was far too little in comparison to the great painfulness of my life.

It was completely disproportionate for one young life to have been so traumatic and problematic, for it to have been such a battle for myself, my friends and family, just so I could become a better person.

My horrendous experiences, both inside my head and outside in the world at large, were far too great for me to be satisfied with the fact that, after all, it had made me learn to improve myself.

Of course that was wonderful, particularly given the massive transformation I have made, but ultimately it wasn't enough. I still subscribed to the belief that I would have been better off never having suffered, and just leading a boring old life like much of the rest of society seemed to.

You know the saying 'Ignorance is Bliss'? That would've done me fine. I would rather have never even encountered an alcoholic, spent my days doing a 9-5 job, having the occasional holiday, living in the rat race, and married to someone I didn't feel massive passion for. I would rather have just settled down, had a plain and uninspiring life, and been one of the 'normies', than have had to deal with the massive pain that my illnesses caused me and others.

I nearly killed myself seven times before I got to where I am now, so it's not an overreaction to say that most of my life has been hellish. So, just becoming a better person and learning some stuff wasn't enough to cut it with me. It wasn't a fair trade at all when you looked at it - and injustice happens to be something I feel very strongly about.

So, let me tell you a little story about how I became the most grateful person in the world for my addiction, and all the other problems it caused. How I became glad of the pain and the suffering, and how I came to the decision that I would never have swapped my life for that of anyone else. How did that miracle happen? Well, I realised what I was born to do.

You see, I have realised what I am here for and it's a mission far greater than I ever would, or could, have imagined - and I am far more passionate about it than I can ever explain. When I first got sober, after being an alcoholic all my adult life (if not being a bit of an alkie child too), I decided I wanted to work in the field. "How great," I thought, "Maybe I could become an addictions counsellor, or something similar, and help other people who are struggling with addiction."

It was a nice thought, and I did go into the addiction field - as an aftercare project co-ordinator. It was great and I loved my job helping others. I loved seeing my clients blossom and bloom and go on to live their lives in recovery. I loved helping people get back into life as the rest of society knows it. But, there still seemed to be something missing.

I was never convinced by the people who said I could use my experience of addiction to help others - as if that was meaning enough. Well, sure I could, but my question remained: "Why did *any* of us have to go through that horrible mess of an experience in the first place?" It didn't make sense. It just seemed like a never-ending cycle of people becoming addicts, some of them recovering their lives, and then going on to help the next generation of addicts to recover *their* lives. What was the point?

It was only later that I realised what it is I was actually *born* to do, and the moment I realised it, quite frankly nothing in heaven or on earth could stop me.

I came to develop a mind-set which means I am now actually grateful for my addiction; for I have come to see that all the things it has given me now far outweigh the awfulness of it. And this is coming from someone who went most of the way down with addiction. I wasn't a heavy drinker or someone who went a bit wild - I am someone who reached very dark and deep places with my addiction and someone who is very lucky to be alive today.

So, eventually I reached that 'transcendental' place; I realised my mission. It is not to help other alcoholics to write a CV, to apply for a college course or to get a job. Some people said I would be suited to counselling, but my mission isn't to spend all my time raking over old feelings either. All those things are wonderful and important, and still a part of what I do, but they're not *my mission*.

My *mission* is to empower recovering addicts to feel the same way that I do about recovery. To help them take the pieces of their lives and create something amazing out of them. I want to change the way that addicts have historically seen themselves. To make them believe in themselves, to become proud of what they have achieved, to stop selling themselves short. I want to help them to and create an amazing life, too. This book is part of that very mission.

But the mission doesn't just stop there, either. Through recovering addicts being proud of themselves and achieving amazing things, I hope to help turn society's stigmatisation of addicts on its head. That is the second part of my mission.

I hope that addicts become recognised for the awesome people they are for overcoming their problems and having the courage to take that forward and go all the way. I hope people will stop seeing addicts as horrible, disgusting, selfish people, and start realising that they are ill. And I hope that we can start promoting a real and widespread celebration of recovery, and recognising all the strength it takes to go through addiction and come out the other side a better person.

It's funny, people think alcoholics and drug addicts have a lack of willpower - ironically, we don't. We are among the most determined people in the world; we just need to learn how to recognise that in ourselves, and use it for the greater good. And that's exactly what we need to show people we can do

Every time I think about my life in terms of my mission, I almost want to cry. Happy, passionate tears these days, not sad ones. What a gift I have been given. None of this can have been accidental - no, it's transcendental. I had my own shed-load of problems so that I can make the world a better bloody place after all. What a wonderful reason for having such a troubled life in the past.

And before anyone starts objecting, wondering if this is flying in the face of the humility that we addicts are all supposed to show, it is absolutely not. Humility is not about shying away from success and from doing great things - humility is about showing the ultimate respect for the life you have and the gifts you have been given. True humility is doing things with others, *for* others, serving the human race in the best way you can. It is not about sitting around on your bum saying you're "too humble" to take up the mantle that has been offered to you.

Humility is about devoting yourself to the greater good. It is about revering the individual lessons and gifts that you have been given and passing them on, rather than keeping them for yourself. There is nothing humble about keeping great things all to yourself. Humility is sharing all you have, not because it's about you, but because it's about who you're giving it to.

So whether you consider yourself to be religious, spiritual, or neither, can you find a greater meaning in your experiences than there ever was in just accepting them, living with them, and trying to look on the bright side? What an amazing gift that is, not just to you but to everyone else. To go beyond yourself and others, and to have a mission in life that is far greater than any one job, or any one person or group. To help other addicts, and by doing that, help to change the fabric of society and the attitude of the world. To bring happiness to individuals and to help make the world a more caring and less judgemental place - what could be better than that? I couldn't dream of any better challenge that I, personally, would like to take on.

I happen to have had certain experiences, and coupled with my own particular qualities, values and skills, I can now see that this was given to me as a chance to help everyone else in the world; not only the addicts - but to help society to become nicer and more understanding, too. Wow, what a mission. And whether I get there, or if I just contribute to making progress, the fact is that I have been given this unique life of mine to do just that, if I choose to.

You will have had different experiences; you will possess different qualities, values and skills from the ones I have. What do they all add up to for you? I would love people to help me on my mission, but you have your own unique life, and so you have to have your own purpose. It may be similar, it may be completely different. It may be unrelated to addiction at all, or it may have some link.

So, I'll ask you the question, what did it feel like to realise what you were born to do?

And if you haven't realised it yet, then get on with the exercises below! There are two of them, and hopefully they'll both take you to the same conclusion; but you just might find you prefer to do one over the other. Do the first one if you like writing on bits of paper, getting up and moving around the room - or the second one if you're a more spiritual person who meditates already. Or do them both and see which gives you the most ideas!

You will know when you have identified your mission, because you'll want to do it more than you have ever wanted to do anything else in your life. It may well be scary or intimidating, or give you moments of self-doubt and fear, but at the same time it will give you a feeling like nothing else in the world. The feeling that this is what you were here to do all along.

There is no need to worry if you don't really understand the methods in the exercises. These are all effective tools, but they can seem a bit strange at first. Just relax and be curious about them.

And don't worry if you don't 'get' your mission at first. Mine didn't come to me immediately. But the techniques below will definitely get your mind moving in the right direction.

As with all of this book, some of the exercises and lessons, will take a little while to master. You are changing your mind, and your life, here. While some things may click in an instant, others will take a while to sink in.

This last bit is the pinnacle of it all, and even if you don't have a mission yet, you can still have a darn fine recovery by doing everything that precedes this chapter. But who knows, you may just be ready to find out what you were born to do, too.

Exercises

From Fruit-bat to Formula

Now lots of us have had those fruit-bat moments, when we think we've discovered something of genius, only for us to eagerly tell one of our mates and then for them to point out a glaring and fatal flaw in our plan. Gah, but it was such a good idea!

Well, what if you could have a bit of a brainstorm, allowing your mind to think up all the genius brainwaves it could, and then you could bypass that embarrassing "Oh yeah" moment when your friends point out to you exactly why something won't work? You can do that bit all by yourself without even having to give your mates the giggles as you tell them of your genius plan.

In fact, you can use this exercise any time that you want to come up with an idea and make it real, but this time we're going to focus on finding out what your mission in life might be.

For this exercise[2] you will need to put four bits of paper on the floor - and be sure to have some extra paper for writing on. So write a different heading on four separate pieces of paper:

1. Realisation
2. Inspired Genius
3. Judge
4. Resolver

Put them around the room in different places on the floor. It doesn't really matter how far apart or where, just make sure that they are far enough apart, so that you won't be standing in the same place when you move between them. A few feet should be enough.

Now go to spot (1) and remember a time when something just dawned on you, when you had that 'Aha!' moment or realised something important. Make it a positive experience if you can. Maybe you'll feel a sense of curiosity, surprise, wonder or joy. Relive that experience fully and feel all the feelings you associate with that state.

Move off the spot and shake yourself out a bit, think of something entirely unrelated. Like what you're having for dinner tonight or how many letters there are in the word 'monumental'.

Next, move onto spot (2) and think of a time when you were able to think and dream in a creative way, when you had ideas uninhibited by niggling details or planning. Just the sparks of great ideas. Most of us have had a time like that as a child when we dreamt of what we might be when we grew up. Relive that experience fully and feel all the feelings you associate with that state.

Move off the spot, shake yourself out, think of something different.

Then move to spot (3) and think of a time when you've been able to objectively pick apart someone else's plan. If you've never done that, imagine what it must feel like to be a judge on X-Factor. And step into the feelings of the 'judge' and really live them fully, taking on the entire mind-set.

Move off the spot, shake yourself out, think of something unrelated.

Finally, move to spot (4) and think of a time when you were able to think in a realistic way, making plans and thinking specifically about moving forward. Think of a time when you were able to bring a lot of threads together, to consolidate a plan of action and to come to a final resolution. Relive that experience and feel the feelings fully. Again, if you can not recall a time you have done that, then imagine what it might be like to experience it.

Now that you've associated each space on the floor with a separate feeling, go through the following steps to formulate your plan of what you could do.

First, go and stand on spot (1) - this is where you are going to think about *what* you want to do. Get back into the mind-set of someone who is having an 'Aha!' moment. Ask yourself the following questions: What are my values? What is the purpose of my life? What positive meaning could I realise through my experiences? How could I use my life to make a difference? What feels right to me? Take as long as you need.

When you've come up with a few ideas, move off the spot, and before you move onto the next spot, shake yourself out, and distract yourself briefly, by thinking of something else.

Next, go and stand on spot (2), get into the state of the 'Inspired Genius' and ask yourself the following questions: What vision do I have of this mission? What would be my ultimate dream? What would I want to see come out of this? How could I fulfil my mission? What options would I take if there were no limits? What would I do if I wasn't afraid? What could the future look like? What do I want to do most of all?

Move off the spot, shake yourself out, think of something unrelated.

Then move to Spot (3) and cast a constructive and critical eye over your genius ideas. Ask yourself: How do I know this will work? Is this a feasible dream for me? What have I missed? Is there a better mission to have? How sure can I be that this will be a success? What else would I need to know? Do I have the resources to get this done? Do I have time to do this?

Move off the spot, shake yourself out, think of something unrelated.

Then move to Spot (4) and start to pull all the threads of what you have learned together into a realistic plan. Get into that realistic, planning mind-set and ask yourself questions such as: What exactly do I need to do? How, specifically, will I implement my ideas? What steps do I need to take? What is the first step?

The beauty of this process is that once you've done it, you can move in between the spots as many times as you need to, finally ending on spot (4) to complete the process.

For example, if on spot (3), the Judge comes up with a "No" in answer to "Is this a feasible dream for me?" then you can always move back to spot (2) again, or even spot (1), and think some more.

The same goes for any of the questions you may become stuck on, or details that you need to work on some more. Just take yourself off to the spot which you think might best help you solve your problem, and do some more thinking!

When you have done this thoroughly, you should find that you have quite a realistic plan, and you should have a certain conviction that it is the right thing to do. And of course, when you have all that, I shouldn't have to remind you by now, it's time to take action. Plan that first step, no matter how small it is - and take it!

Or if you're still stuck, try the second exercise...

Ask your 'Wise Mind'

There is a part of you that is the wisest part of all. Believe it or not, it is neither the part that knows how to work out complicated mathematical problems, nor the part that is defined purely by your emotions. It is actually that part of you that just 'knows' when something is right. It's a lovely balance between the two - the logic and the emotion.

This part of you tends not to come about when rushed, or pressured or backed into a corner, but when you give it the space to really combine the two parts of you; the creative, more emotional side and the reasonable side.

So-called 'Wise Mind' is born of the overlapping of the intellectual, rational side and the emotional, feeling side. It could be described as intuition or a sense of what is right.

Some people feel this 'knowing' as an actual sensation in their body, like a 'gut feeling' or something their 'heart' tells them. Do not mistake it for doing what you emotionally feel is right - Wise Mind has a different feeling. It is true and centred.

The physical feelings of Wise Mind are sometimes accompanied by another feeling - of certainty, calmness or wisdom. Even if you are making a difficult choice when using Wise Mind, there is a part of you that stays reassured because you know it's the right thing to do.

Some of you are probably familiar with the Serenity Prayer:

"Grant me the serenity to accept

the things I can not change,

the courage to change the things I can,

and the wisdom to know the difference."

Wise Mind is something similar to that last line - it knows when change or acceptance is necessary.

People do not necessarily know how to automatically tune into their wisest part, but it is something that can be cultivated with practice. And the good news is that everyone has this part of them - they just need to know how to access it.

So, first of all I will give you an exercise, so that you can practise finding your Wise Mind, and then when you think you may have got there, you can ask yourself that question: "What is my mission to be?"

Practising Wise Mind

1. Take a mental pause and empty your mind.

2. Count to 10 and then take a deep breath in.

3. As you start to breathe out, pay attention to your breath and follow it, rising all the way from your lungs to your nose or mouth.

4. When you have fully exhaled, follow your in-breath, feeling it filling your body.

5. Keep breathing like this and following your breath until you feel calm. If it helps, you can either count your breaths to retain focus on them, or think to yourself 'in' on the in-breath and 'out' on the out-breath.

6. Open your awareness, becoming open to sensations, instincts and feelings.

7. Let the focus of your attention go to the bottom of your in-breath.

8. Still focussing there, ask yourself a question and listen out for an awareness of the answer.

Don't rush in and mentally answer the question. Instead wait until an answer comes that is true. It may not even come in words.

Some practice questions you can ask yourself to see if you have located your Wise Mind might be: "What do I know?" "Who am I?" "What do I need?"

Now you can test to see if your answer truly comes from Wise Mind, by asking yourself if the answer is truly right for you, and if it would be right at any time. If you practise this exercise every day, you will come to know what your Wise Mind feels like and you can trust it.

And once you have found your Wise Mind and are comfortable with it, remember to ask it the most important question of all! What is your mission or the meaning of your journey? When you think you have that, you can also ask some of the questions in the first exercise to bring more clarity to your mission, and to how you might best accomplish it.

Take-aways:

- Your life will be even happier if you can find a purpose and a mission
- Missions are all about a greater meaning
- It is not humble to keep your gifts to yourself
- Your true mission will set your soul on fire!

"Here is the test to find whether your mission on Earth is finished: if you're alive, it isn't."

- Richard Bach

Chapter Fifteen

Clean Pride, Anyone?

I would hope that if this book has taught you anything, it has taught you to stop thinking about yourself and your life in limiting ways.

You are not '*just* an addict' - and you are more than capable of living an amazing life and being a power of good in the world. You are more than capable of using your own special gifts to contribute to others, and to teach. You have learnt that you have been influenced by your experiences in positive ways, and that you do not have to be limited by your past, or stuck in your old patterns. You have learnt how you can have not just a strong recovery, but an *amazing* recovery, where you are practising certain behaviours to accelerate your happiness and your growth as a person.

You have recognised that you are powerful beyond measure - from the strength you have that bore you through addiction and recovery, to the power you have to change and develop your life from now on.

I don't mean you're an egomaniac who thinks that you are an omnipotent being with the power to control everything - this is more about the power of personal choice than anything else. And I don't care if you call it your own power, a 'Higher Power' or just common sense and psychology - the truth is, you have it. And it's yours to keep and cherish.

You have taken the time to read this book and to invest in your own life. And I would like you to thank yourself for taking your experience in the spirit it was intended - to teach you, to learn, to become a better person, to see yourself as a special person in your own right, to become uniquely you.

And the next thing I would suggest to you is to be proud of who you are. Decide you're not scared any more, as you start to live the principles in this book.

Now I'm not necessarily suggesting that you go around shouting about your recovery if you don't want to just yet, but I'd like you at least to be proud in yourself, and hold that in your heart.

It just so happens that I am entirely open about my own recovery and that's because I have learnt to see it not as a failing, but a reason for celebration. And I am open for the sake of other addicts who are trying to get well. The way I see it, who is going to want to recover when everyone else that has recovered is hiding away?

If certain people along my journey had not disclosed to me about their own journey, I might never be where I am now. I might have thought recovery was impossible, or that it was not worth attaining. After all if no-one is prepared to stand up and show other addicts how great it is, how would *I* have ever known?

I know that society has stigmatised people with mental health and addiction problems, but if no-one is going to announce to the world that having been an addict is not a shameful failing, but an illness that they have overcome, how on Earth is society ever expected to change? We can not expect ignorance to just disappear if we are not prepared to challenge it ourselves.

So, I am asking some of you to be brave and to share your stories as much as you feel comfortable with. It is up to you how far you want to go with this and I'm not suggesting that everyone is in the right space to reveal all about their addiction just yet. But if you are, then do celebrate recovery!

My approach is to live my recovery, to talk about it, to write about it, and to make it part of my business; and my mission is to spread the word.

I am careful to point out that while I have an amazing recovery, it does not mean I will *never* relapse. Unfortunately, relapse can still happen when you least expect it. It is part of the illness. While I hope all my relapses are behind me, I will not put myself in danger by dismissing the possibility out of hand, because who knows what the future holds? But I am very public about my recovery being fantastic and strong at this point in my life, and I have every reason to believe that it will be so for a long time to come, as I continue to do the right things, and to create a dynamic present and a compelling future.

Not everyone will be at the point where they want to be as open as I am, and I understand that too. Some of you will be scared about how it might affect your families or your jobs - and I know that the world doesn't change its mind overnight.

But at this very moment in time, it is becoming easier than ever before to share your recovery, as people are becoming more open about their struggles; and there is indeed a Recovery Movement growing, of which I am grateful to be a part.

Do you remember the days when being gay was considered a crime, or when different races were routinely oppressed? If people hadn't stood up, spoken out and taken action to end things, then nothing would have changed. This is the way it is with mental health issues these days - people who haven't experienced it can be scared, ignorant or just plain insensitive.

The power to change society must lie with the group affected. Therefore I see it as my responsibility to speak out. Again, it might not necessarily be fair, but it is the reality, and so I will take on the challenge I have been given.

Some non-addicts might read the preceding paragraph, and think it is somewhat dramatic; but I can not tell you how many times I have been misunderstood and treated like an idiot, a piece of dirt, or worse, by other people because of my illness. This misunderstanding and disrespect has been shown to me, not only by members of the general public, but also by professionals, including doctors and other medical staff, who I would have hoped to be better informed and more understanding. I am sure most addicts can relate encounters where an ignorant and hostile attitude has been taken against them, including cases where this has directly harmed them.

So, if you're coming on board, make a list of all the ways you might be able to help the cause of de-stigmatising addicts, helping more of us to be able to ask for help, and to recover. This is essentially what it is all about in the end. Addicts suffer for much longer than they need to, because they are often too scared and ashamed to ask for help when they suspect they might have an issue. And that is directly due to stigma.

So, could you talk at a local school or university? Could you write an article for your local paper? Could you join a Celebrate Recovery group or meet-up? Or go on a Recovery Walk?

Or maybe you could share the message in a way that doesn't identify you quite so publicly as an addict, if that is still a complex issue for you. Maybe you could write a few letters to newspapers anonymously, sign a few petitions, write to your MP about addiction, support some relevant charities. Or if you hear people ignorantly talking about addicts in a disparaging way, you could just quietly correct them.

Do what you can, *if* you can to spread the message, without putting yourself and those around you at risk. The more of us who do what we can, in large ways or small, to promote the message that it's not shameful to suffer from the illness of addiction, and that we can recover, the easier it will be for future generations to ask for help. And I am all for that.

And if there is anything I can do to make your path easier or to help you to share the message, then please do not hesitate to let me know.

Some of you won't be ready yet and some of you may feel it is not right for you. And that's OK too. If you can't share the message out loud just yet, I'd like you at least to keep the message within yourself that you *are* proud of who you are.

I am proud of all of you who have got well, who are trying to get well, who are battling through, and who are sharing your journeys. It is a difficult path to be given in life, but it is one of the most rewarding, if you let it be.

Take-aways:

- Go get 'em, tiger!

No more quotations, no more exercises. Just go out in the world and live. Be happy being you, doing the right thing, living your values, loving your life and helping others.

Afterword

If you haven't noticed already the title to this book is kind of a play on words. If you live by the principles in this book, you will find that you are not only a happier recovering alcoholic or drug addict, but you might just find that you become addicted to happiness too.

We can all be addicts in healthy ways as well as non-healthy ways. An addiction means that you want more of something, that you feel compelled to have more of it in your life from day to day - and I don't think that's a bad thing when it comes to happiness.

As you will remember from the chapter on neuroplasticity, the more you train your brain to be happy, the happier you will become.

This is true of everything you do - at first it may seem like a bit of an effort, but the more you behave in the right ways and make the right choices, the more effortless it becomes. Positive thinking does become automatic in the end, so it really is worth investing some time in deliberately changing how you think, and what you think about.

If this book has helped you, please spread the word among the grumpier addicts that you know. Recovery is a wonderful place if you let it be, and I'd like all of us in recovery to be as happy as possible. We didn't get better just to be miserable. Here's to your happiness!

References

1. This analysis is based on data from the 2001-2002 *National Epidemiologic Survey on Alcohol and Related Conditions* (NESARC), a project of the National Institutes of Health's National Institute on Alcohol Abuse and Alcoholism (NIAAA).

2. With thanks to Robert Dilts, NLP pioneer. This technique is based on The Disney Strategy, a strategy which he formulated after studying how Walt Disney came up with such fantastic, but realistic, ideas.

Dilts' book *Strategies of Genius Vol. 1* details the original pattern, which I have changed fairly dramatically, but I thought it right to acknowledge him as he pioneered a lot of NLP techniques.

List of Values

Accountability	Achievement	Adventure
Altruism	Ambition	Assertiveness
Balance	Belonging	Boldness
Calmness	Carefulness	Caring
Challenge	Cheerfulness	Clarity
Commitment	Community	Compassion
Competitiveness	Congruity	Consistency
Contentment	Contribution	Control
Cooperation	Creativity	Curiosity
Decisiveness	Dependability	Determination
Development	Diligence	Discipline
Diversity	Dynamism	Effectiveness
Efficiency	Empathy	Enjoyment
Enthusiasm	Excellence	Excitement
Expressiveness	Fairness	Faith

Family
Freedom
Generosity
Grace
Happiness
Health
Honour
Ingenuity
Intelligence
Irreverence
Kindness
Legacy
Making a difference
Openness
Overcoming
Positivity
Professionalism
Resourcefulness
Selflessness
Serenity
Spontaneity
Striving
Support
Thoroughness
Traditionalism
Understanding
Usefulness
Wisdom

Fidelity
Frivolity
Giving
Gratitude
Hard Work
Helping Others
Humility
Inquisitiveness
Intellectualism
Joy
Leadership
Love
Mastery
Order
Perfection
Practicality
Prudence
Security
Self-reliance
Service
Stability
Structure
Teamwork
Thoughtfulness
Trustworthiness
Uniqueness
Vision

Focus
Fun
Goodness
Growth
Harmony
Honesty
Independence
Insightfulness
Intuition
Justice
Learning
Loyalty
Obedience
Originality
Piety
Preparedness
Reliability
Self-control
Sensitivity
Simplicity
Strength
Success
Temperance
Tolerance
Truth
Unity
Vitality

Printed in Great Britain
by Amazon